MW01601252

TM

Adult
Bible Study Series

By Thomas J. Doyle

Portions of the "Study" and "Apply" sections
were written by Carl C. Fickenscher II

"Catechism Connections" were written
by Arnold Schmidt

CONCORDIA PUBLISHING HOUSE • SAINT LOUIS

Contents

Introduction

God promises to strengthen our life in Christ as we study His Word. The Our Life in Christ Bible Study series provides you resources to help you study God's Word. The series gives you an opportunity to study in depth some familiar, and possibly not-so-familiar, biblical accounts.

Each of the nine Bible study books has 13 sessions that are divided into four easy-to-use sections.

Gather—Section 1 of each session points participants to the key concept for the session.

Study—Section 2 of each session explores a portion of Scripture through the use of a brief commentary and questions that help the participants study the text.

Apply—Section 3 of each session helps the participants apply to their lives both God's Law and Gospel revealed in the scriptural account.

Send—Section 4 of each session provides the participants with practical suggestions for taking the theme of the lesson out of the classroom and into the world.

Our Life in Christ is designed to assist both novice and expert Bible students with resources that will enable them to grow in their understanding of God's Word while strengthening their life in Christ.

As an added benefit, the sessions in the Our Life in Christ Adult Bible Study series follow the Scripture lessons taught in the Our Life in Christ Sunday school series. Parents will enjoy studying in depth the Bible stories their children are studying in Sunday school. This will provide parents with opportunities to

- discuss God's Word together;
- extend lesson applications to everyday situations;
- pray together; and
- engage in family activities that grow out of the lesson truths.

We pray that as you study God's Word using the Our Life in Christ Adult Bible Study series, your life in Christ may be strengthened.

Adult Study Guide

World History	Dates	Biblical People
Neo-Sumerian	2000 B.C.	
Egypt, New Kingdom	1500 B.C.	
Philistine Invasion	1000 B.C.	
Assyrian Empire	785 B.C.	
Old Testament Ends	430 B.C.	
Roman Empire		
	c. A.D. 30	Jesus Christ Pilate
	c. A.D. 33	Stephen
	c. A.D. 60	Paul

Jesus Talks about Greatness

(Matthew 18:1–9; 20:17–28)

Gather

Theme: Who Is the Greatest?

Key Point

Jesus demonstrated greatness to us when He willingly gave Himself to death on the cross. His servant greatness on our behalf motivates us to serve Him and others.

Objectives

By the power of the Holy Spirit working through God's Word, we will

1. compare Jesus' description of greatness with the world's concept of greatness;
2. confess our sinful selfishness that would cause us to seek greatness through our own efforts and merits;
3. affirm the forgiveness Jesus won for our self-centeredness when He emptied Himself of His glory and suffered and died on the cross; and
4. joyfully respond to Jesus' servant love by serving God and others.

Opening

Read in unison the Second Article of the Apostles' Creed and Luther's explanation.

[I believe] in Jesus Christ, His only Son, our Lord, who was conceived by the Holy Spirit, born of the Virgin Mary, suffered under Pontius Pilate, was crucified, died, and was buried.

He descended into hell. The third day He rose again from the dead. He ascended into heaven and sits at the right hand of God, the Father Almighty. From thence He will come to judge the living and the dead.

What does this mean? I believe that Jesus Christ, true God, begotten of the Father from eternity, and also true man, born of the Virgin Mary, is my Lord, who has redeemed me, a lost and condemned person, purchased and won me from all sins, from death, and from the power of the devil; not with gold or silver, but with His holy, precious blood and with His innocent suffering and death, that I may be His own, and live under Him in His kingdom and serve Him in everlasting righteousness, innocence, and blessedness, just as He is risen from the dead, lives and reigns to all eternity.

This is most certainly true.

Introduction

"Who's the greatest?"

1. If you were asked to identify "great" people, whom would you choose? Why?

2. What qualities and characteristics does a "great" person have?

In today's session Jesus answers the question "Who's the greatest?" in two separate events. In both events Jesus smashes traditional views of greatness and affirms that true greatness only comes through Him who makes people great before God through His sacrificial life, death, and glorious resurrection.

Study

Read aloud Matthew 18:1–9 and 20:17–28.

Reading the Text

"Who is the greatest in the kingdom of heaven?" the disciples ask. Jesus answered that question often in His ministry. Today's stories are just two of the occasions on which Jesus corrected misunderstandings about true greatness.

In both of today's incidents, the issue of greatness comes up shortly after Jesus has spoken of His death. The first, according to Matthew's account (Matthew 18:1–9; notice 17:22–23), begins with the disciples' question, "Who is the greatest?" The gospel according to Mark reports that, prior to asking this question, the disciples had been disputing this issue as they traveled to Capernaum (Mark 9:33–34). Jesus turns the tables by asking the disciples a question about the nature of their discussion. In response, they hang their heads in silence and shame. Jesus now has a teachable moment.

A little child provides the ideal illustration (Matthew 18:2–6). The important question, Jesus suggests, is not who will be greatest in the kingdom of heaven, but whether one will enter it at all. And that happens only when the Holy Spirit creates faith in a person's heart so that he believes in Jesus with childlike trust. Children, of course, are dependent on others for all things. Likewise, faith in Christ—the only means by which anyone may enter heaven—requires an understanding that one is helpless before God, totally dependent on Him for salvation.

Children, therefore, are models of faith, and are far better examples of faith than adults who contend for personal glory. "Little ones" can and do believe in Jesus through the Holy Spirit's work. It is, in fact, a grievous sin, worthy of drowning "in the depths of the sea," to come between a child and Christ.

The perfect example of one who humbles himself is Jesus. Clearly Jesus is reminding His disciples that the greatest in the kingdom of heaven is the One who emptied Himself of all glory and humbled Himself even to the death of the cross (Philippians 2:5–11).

By contrast, anything that causes someone to fall away from faith—for example, pride or lust for earthly power—must be "cut

11

off" or "gouged out" (Matthew 18:7–9). Jesus is not literally commanding physical mutilation, for it is never really the hand or foot or eye that causes a person to sin. Rather, He is saying that nothing in life is worth having if one has to forfeit eternal life for it.

The second incident follows Jesus' most explicit reference to His approaching passion. To His previous prophecies of suffering (e.g., 16:21; 17:9; and 17:22), Jesus now adds the details of mocking and scourging by the Gentiles and, most important, crucifixion (20:17–19).

What a time for the disciples to be worried about personal honors! Yet James and John ("the sons of Zebedee") with their mother, Salome, come to ask just that of Jesus (20:20–28). (Comparing Matthew's description with Mark 10:35–45 indicates that the disciples "seconded" their mother's request.)

Some people in Jesus' day envisioned the heavenly kingdom to be much like an earthly one, with certain people holding more exalted positions than others. Having recognized Jesus as the heavenly king, a mother and her sons wish to put in an early bid for seats at either side of His throne (Matthew 20:21). Interestingly, Jesus does not dispel this throne-room imagery (20:23).

He does, however, teach that the nature of the kingdom is quite different. Are James and John interested in sharing what Jesus' kingdom involves? In fact, *can* they? "The cup" was a familiar expression for suffering, especially suffering God's wrath (Psalm 75:8; Jeremiah 25:15–29; and, later, Matthew 26:39). Naively, the two disciples say yes: they will gladly put up with whatever inconvenience they must tolerate. How exciting, they may even have thought, to be gallant heroes, struggling alongside their Master!

Certainly they have no idea what they are asking. Bearing Jesus' "cup" will not mean achieving a heroic, hard-fought victory with a few wounds and deprivations. It will mean enduring a brutal, violent defeat. It will mean suffering the very anguish of hell for the sins of the world. (In Mark's gospel, Jesus also asks whether James and John can share His "baptism," recalling that Jesus took our place under sin when He was baptized in the Jordan. See Mark 10:38.) Indeed, the disciples and all Christians do share in Jesus' suffering, but even this is not to be taken as a means of gaining honor (Matthew 20:23).

Instead, true greatness is marked by service that seeks nothing for itself (Matthew 20:24–28). Jesus explains to all 12 disciples that His kingdom will not be like that of the Gentiles, where power denotes greatness: for the disciples, the greatest will be the greatest servant. Paradoxically, those who *wish* to be first, seeking their own glory, will be last—as slaves. Those who willingly seek to serve others will, quite to their surprise, ultimately find themselves counted among the greats.

Once more, all of this points to Christ Himself. The One who deserved to be served by all chose to become the suffering servant (Isaiah 52:13–53:12). His life became the ransom that bought back—redeemed—all people from slavery.

Discussing the Text

1. Note the evidence of the disciples' pride and ambition in both incidents (Matthew 18:1–9; 20:17–28). What added insight do you find in Mark's account (9:33–34)?

2. How does a little child provide an ideal illustration of Jesus' teaching about greatness?

3. How is Jesus the perfect example of one who humbles Himself?

4. How do James and John's personal desires for greatness (Matthew 20:21) indicate that they do not properly understand the nature of the kingdom of God?

5. Paraphrase Jesus' description of true greatness (20:25–28). How much appreciation for such greatness have you seen in the world today?

Apply

Just as worldly greatness was a recurring issue with Jesus' disciples, so we all too often engage in selfish rivalries, jealousies, and unwholesome competition. We want to be head of the line, the boss's favorite, or able to tell a better story.

Jesus' solution is *not*, as it might seem, to encourage us to strive for greatness by trying to be the best servants. That would in fact be nothing but redirecting the same selfish objectives. Rather, Jesus offers Himself. His servanthood is, of course, the model to be followed. But far beyond that, as we realize more and more how we have been served by Christ, we will in spontaneous gratitude look for ways to build up others, encourage our friends, and support other people.

In applying this lesson, we need to confess our selfishness. The humble servanthood that we desire will grow from the assurance of forgiveness given freely by Christ.

1. How do our thoughts, words, and actions often demonstrate self-centeredness?

2. Jesus doesn't encourage us to strive for greatness by becoming the best servants. How instead does Jesus empower us for servanthood?

3. Why is it important to confess our sinful self-centeredness? What does Jesus provide to all who confess their sins? How does that which Jesus provides result in a life of servanthood?

4. What insights to servanthood do you find in Ephesians 2:1–10?

Catechism Connection

Examine the Second Article and Martin Luther's explanation in the opening for this session.

1. Note especially Luther's words, "who has redeemed me, a lost and condemned person, purchased and won me from all sins, from death, and from the power of the devil." Which of these same truths did you find in Ephesians 2:1–10?

2. From what three things has Christ redeemed us according to John 8:34–36, 1 Corinthians 15:55–57; and 1 John 3:8?

Send

To Do This Week

Family Connection

1. Discuss with your family the topic of greatness. Ask, "What are the characteristics of a 'great' person?" Then compare the characteristics of greatness with the characteristics Jesus demonstrated.

2. Considering Jesus' example of greatness—laying down His life for all people—discuss how you can demonstrate this kind of greatness to family members, friends, and acquaintances.

3. Examine the hymn "How Great Thou Art" (*LW* 519). Talk about the greatness revealed in stanza 3.

For Personal Reflection

1. Pray that God would enable you to demonstrate greatness to others as you serve them and God.

2. Reread the Second Article of the Apostles' Creed and Luther's explanation as part of your personal devotions. Meditate on the magnitude of God's love for you demonstrated in the person and work of Jesus.

3. Demonstrate a servant attitude toward someone this week who considers greatness something he or she has to work to acquire.

For Next Week

Read Matthew 21:1–11 and 27:45–66 in preparation for the next session.

Session 2

Jesus Enters Jerusalem

(Matthew 21:1–11; 27:45–66)

Gather

Theme: His Primary Purpose

Key Point

Jesus' primary purpose in coming to earth was to die on a cross for the sins of all people so that we could receive God's free gifts of forgiveness of sins and eternal life.

Objectives

By the power of the Holy Spirit working through God's Word, we will

1. explain how the events of Palm Sunday set the stage for the events leading up to Jesus' arrest, trial, and crucifixion;
2. describe the primary purpose of Jesus coming to earth; and
3. share the meaning of Jesus' death for our lives.

Opening

Read the Second Commandment and Martin Luther's explanation responsively.

All: You shall not misuse the name of the Lord your God.

Leader: What does this mean?

Participants: We should fear and love God so that we do not curse, swear, use satanic arts, lie, or deceive by His name, but call upon it in every trouble, pray, praise, and give thanks.

Introduction

1. What is the primary purpose for each of the following: a waiter in a restaurant?

   a comedian?

   a physician?

   a parent?

   a teacher?

2. What was the primary purpose for Jesus coming to earth?

3. What is the primary purpose of the Christian church?

    In today's session we will see that many people misunderstood Jesus' primary purpose for coming to earth, and we will examine why a proper understanding of His purpose was essential for the people of Jesus' day and remains essential for people today.

Study

Read aloud Matthew 21:1–11 and 27:45–66.

Reading the Text

    Jesus' triumphal entry into Jerusalem is often seen as a near-success that fell just short. One day Jesus is welcomed into the city by adoring crowds; less than a week later He is condemned to death. We may think that, if only the same crowds had not turned against Him, perhaps the tragedy of the cross could have been avoided. Nothing could be further from the truth. Jesus came to Jerusalem for one purpose only: to die. The triumphal entry was in no way a failed attempt at glory for Christ; rather, it was a very successful step toward suffering.

It is the week of Passover, when crowds of faithful Jews are streaming toward Jerusalem. Jesus' last stop with His disciples is the home of Martha, Mary, and Lazarus (John 12:1), the same Lazarus whom Jesus had raised from the dead earlier (John 11:1–46). Their home is in Bethany, on the eastern slope of the Mount of Olives, a scant two miles east of Jerusalem.

Knowing exactly what must take place, Jesus sends two disciples ahead to Bethphage, a small village even closer to Jerusalem, just down the road that leads into the city (Matthew 21:1–3). He assures them that they will find a donkey and her colt and that they will be permitted to take the animals for the Lord. Jesus initiates and directs everything that will happen this day. Luke emphasizes that the disciples found everything in Bethphage "just as He had told them" (Luke 19:32). And Matthew underscores that Jesus' plans are just as the prophets had long foretold (Matthew 21:4–5; Isaiah 62:11; Zechariah 9:9). Jesus mounts the colt—its mother would naturally follow behind—and begins His ride toward the city (Matthew 21:6–7).

The crowd of Passover visitors, perhaps those from Galilee especially, has been hoping for this occasion. Many had already gathered near Lazarus' house, eager to see both Jesus and the one He had raised from the dead (John 12:9). Now, spurred by Jesus' action, they come rushing out to meet Him (John 12:12–13, 17–19). Laying coats in the road and waving branches were both traditional signs of welcome for a king (2 Kings 9:13; Revelation 7:9–10). Only John's gospel specifies that the branches were palm branches.

The crowds know what Jesus' arrival means: He is King, the Messiah. Among their shouts (Matthew 21:9) are words from one of the greatest messianic psalms (Psalm 118:25–26). "Hosanna" is a prayer that literally means, "Save now!" God's people had waited many years for the Son of David, the Blessed One from the Lord, to come and reestablish the kingdom of their father David. They are more than ready for Him to save now! His arrival will even bring "peace in heaven and glory in the highest" (Luke 19:38). It is significant that Luke records these shouts, because they echo the words of the angels at Jesus' birth (Luke 2:14).

The procession travels down the western slope of the Mount of Olives, into the deep Kidron Valley, and then up the steep eastern ascent of Mount Zion on which Jerusalem and the temple are built. Amid the wild enthusiasm, perhaps few noticed Jesus suddenly break into tears (Luke 19:41–44). Only Jesus could fully see beyond the excitement of the moment to the tragedies ahead—His rejection by Jerusalem and its subsequent destruction by the Romans in A.D. 70.

The euphoria carries Jesus through the city gates and into the temple. Now even routine commerce stops as the whole city is caught up in the buzz. Jesus' enemies are furious at the disturbance, but nothing can stop it. It is a glorious moment!

Yet Jesus knows the real purpose of His coming. He enters the city as King, but not as the king most of the people want. The prophet Zechariah relates God's purpose: the King comes humbly, riding on a donkey, not a mighty warhorse. He comes not to conquer earthly enemies for Israel, but to cut off the chariot and bow in order to establish eternal, spiritual peace for *all* nations (Zechariah 9:9–10).

Peace will be achieved only by the King's ultimate humiliation. The "triumphal entry" must always be viewed in the light of—or, rather, the darkness of—Good Friday (Matthew 27:45–66). Just five days after Palm Sunday, Jesus will hang on the cross. Darkness will cover the land from noon until 3:00 P.M., and Jesus will be rejected by everyone, including the crowds who shouted, "Hosanna." Even the heavenly Father will be forced to forsake His Son, turning His back, withdrawing all His protection, so that Jesus suffers the very torments of damnation.

Still, Palm Sunday has not been a terrible misunderstanding. The signs at Jesus' death—the earthquake, the ripping of the temple curtain, the resurrection of the saints, even the words of the Roman officer in charge (27:51–54)—testify that Jesus is truly the One who has come in the name of the Lord. The triumphal entry was simply not intended as the final, crowning achievement.

Discussing the Text

1. For what purpose did Jesus come to Jerusalem, and ultimately, to the earth? See Matthew 16:21–23; 17:11–12, 22–23; and 20:17–19.

2. How would you explain Jesus' triumphal entry into Jerusalem on Sunday and His suffering and death only five days later?

3. What is the meaning of the crowd shouting "Hosanna" (21:9)? In what sense might their words have had more meaning than they intended?

4. How did Jesus' enemies react to His entry into Jerusalem (21:15)?

5. How did the people misunderstand the real purpose of Jesus' coming to earth?

Apply

Palm Sunday is a wonderful opportunity to focus on the chief purpose of Jesus' coming to earth. Every Sunday we hear something important and gracious that Jesus has done: miracles, healing and caring for people, and teaching God's wisdom. We have the clear understanding that Jesus is the "star" of our Sunday school and our Bible class. But Jesus is not rightly understood if His "star quality" is seen as primary. Jesus did not come to be "like Mike" (Michael Jordan) or other celebrities, with spotlights and endorsements and cheering crowds. That was the misunderstanding of many in the Palm Sunday parade.

Jesus came to be the last guy on the bench, the One who does nothing except help the team win. Jesus' purpose was to be stripped of all glory, to suffer the rejection of all, the punishments of hell. Jesus came riding into Jerusalem to die. We see the cross as, finally, *the* reason Jesus came to earth. Everything else we teach depends on this truth: "I resolved to know nothing while I was with you except Jesus Christ and Him crucified" (1 Corinthians 2:2).

1. How do some people today misunderstand the purpose of Jesus' coming to earth? Consider the following statements:

"Jesus was a great prophet."

"Jesus taught us how to live."

"Jesus came to give us an example of moral living."

2. Why is it important that we affirm that His death was Jesus' primary purpose for coming to earth? See Hebrews 2:14.

3. If death was Jesus' primary purpose for coming to earth, why do we study His miracles, His teaching, and His life?

4. Why does the primary message of the Christian church need to remain always "Jesus Christ crucified"? See 1 Corinthians 1:18 and 2:2.

5. Share the meaning of Christ's crucifixion for your life.

Catechism Connection

Examine the Second Commandment and Luther's explanation in the opening for this session.

1. What evils of society are condemned in Leviticus 19:31 and Ecclesiastes 7:14?

2. Why do you think people resort to these sins so easily and so often?

3. What better advice does God offer in Psalm 50:15?

Send

To Do This Week

Family Connection

1. Review the events of the Palm Sunday account. Discuss why it was appropriate for people to sing "Hosanna."

2. Create a family "Hosanna" poster or banner to hang in your home.

3. Share with each other what Jesus' death means for your life.

For Personal Reflection

1. Meditate on the magnitude of God's love for you revealed in Jesus' primary purpose for coming to earth.

2. Share with a friend or a loved one the meaning of Jesus' death for your life.

3. Read the entire Passion account from beginning to end (Matthew 26:1–27:66).

For Next Week

Read Matthew 26:57–66 in preparation for next week's session.

Session 3

Church Leaders Condemn Jesus

(Matthew 26:57–66)

Gather

Theme: The Tables Are Turned!

Key Point

Because of God's love for us the tables are turned: Jesus received God's judgment and punishment for our sin, and we receive the blessing of forgiveness of sins and eternal life. His love enables us to turn the tables for others who are lost in their sins.

Objectives

By the power of the Holy Spirit working through God's Word, we will

1. recount the events leading up to Jesus' crucifixion;
2. describe the unfair treatment of Jesus at the hearings before the religious and government leaders;
3. confess our sin and receive the assurance of the forgiveness and eternal life won for us through Jesus' death on the cross; and
4. share the story of how God turned the tables for us.

Opening

Read the Eighth Commandment and Martin Luther's explanation responsively.

All: You shall not give false testimony against your neighbor.

Leader: What does this mean?

Participants: We should fear and love God so that we do not tell lies about our neighbor, betray him, slander him, or hurt his reputation, but defend him, speak well of him, and explain everything in the kindest way.

Introduction

"The tables are turned."

1. What situation might cause you or someone you know to speak these words?

2. How did God's love for us in Jesus "turn the tables" for us and our fate?

In the familiar events of the passion, God turns the tables for us as He declares us "Not guilty" because His Son received the punishment we deserved.

Study

Read aloud Matthew 26:57–66.

Reading the Text

Opposition to Jesus grows. His enemies make a desperate play to destroy Him. Jesus will be arrested, tried, and killed, but, as He promised, He will rise again on the third day. His resurrection will be preached by His disciples to the world.

The so-called "trial" before Caiaphas is actually just the second of five questionings Jesus endured that night and morning. The first two were conducted by the religious authorities, the last three by Roman government officials. After being arrested in the garden, Jesus was first taken to Annas, the former high priest and father-in-law of Caiaphas (John 18:12–13). Next Jesus faced Caiaphas himself. It was these religious leaders, such as Annas and Caiaphas, who wished to kill Jesus. Since the Jewish people were subject to Rome, however, only Roman officials could execute a man (John 18:31). The priests and elders therefore brought Jesus to Pilate, the Roman governor of Judea (Matthew 27:1–2). After a brief examination, though, hoping to avoid responsibility, Pilate sent Jesus to Herod Antipas, the Roman puppet ruler of Galilee, who also happened to be in Jerusalem for the feast (Luke 23:1–12). Finally, Herod returned Jesus to Pilate, who passed the fateful sentence (Matthew 27:11–26).

It was before Caiaphas, nevertheless, that the real point at issue was spoken. Caiaphas was one of seven men of Annas's family (five sons and a grandson besides Caiaphas) to sit as high priest. Caiaphas was of the Sadducee party (see Matthew 22:23; Acts 23:6–8), but he seems to have shown little genuine religious conviction. He was coldly convinced that Jesus must die in order to protect what little power Rome had granted the nation (John 11:47–53).

The proceedings before Caiaphas cannot truly be called a trial, because it was not a formally called meeting of the Sanhedrin, the Jewish ruling council. Only 23 of the council's 71 members were required for a quorum, but even with a select minimum present, so many blatant violations of the law could never have been tolerated in an official meeting. For example, such serious cases could only be tried in the regular council chamber, not in the high priest's palace (Luke 22:54). Moreover no trial could begin at night or be held on the eve of a feast day. Obviously, Jesus' enemies wanted secrecy. Perhaps men like Joseph of Arimathea and Nicodemus were excluded (Luke 23:50–53; John 3:1–2; 7:45–51; 19:38–39).

Rather than a formal conviction, the purpose of the hearing was twofold: first, to ease the consciences of as many leaders as possible, and, second, to find charges that could carry the death sentence in Roman court. (Pilate, the religious leaders knew, would never crucify Jesus over "religious" issues.)

Thus they paraded false witnesses (Matthew 26:59–61), looking for any two who would agree (as required by law; Deuteronomy

17:6; 19:15). Their best effort was two witnesses who misquoted Jesus' words, "Destroy this temple, and I will raise it again in three days" (John 2:19; see also Matthew 27:39–40 and Acts 6:13–14). Not only were they quoting Jesus out of context (for He had been speaking of the destruction and resurrection of His body, not the physical temple), but the very words they cited were inaccurate. Jesus had said that they—not He—would destroy the "temple." Remarkably, even these witnesses did not agree (Mark 14:59), so clumsy and obviously trumped-up were the charges.

Jesus would dignify none of this with a word. Knowing His mission, He was willing to suffer in silence (see Isaiah 53:7).

Finally, having failed to discover any political charges to bring to the Romans, Caiaphas must resort to the real issue: Jesus' teaching. He puts Jesus under oath, which, according to Scripture, required Jesus to respond (Leviticus 5:1). "Tell us if You are the Christ, the Son of God," Caiaphas demands. Caiaphas' command demonstrates how clear and open Jesus' teachings and ministry have been; Caiaphas knows what Jesus will say.

Jesus' answer, literally "You have said it," is not evasive. It is actually definitive, pointing out what Caiaphas himself has known all along. (Mark's account has the most emphatic expression, "I am," a response that echoes God's Old Testament personal name, I AM. See Exodus 3:13–15.) Jesus then adds two quotations that refer to the Messiah (Psalm 110:1 and Daniel 7:13–14). These passages are ironic—and surely bitter to Caiaphas—because they describe the final court of judgment. One day the tables will be turned; Jesus will sit in judgment with all people at His feet!

Caiaphas pronounces his verdict: "He has spoken blasphemy!" Blasphemy is any speech that ridicules God. Caiaphas charges Jesus with mocking God by saying that God was a mere man— Jesus Himself. Though the high priest was ordinarily forbidden to tear his clothes (Leviticus 10:6; 21:10), custom required him to do so in cases of blasphemy. (Tearing open one's loose, outer robe was a common expression of great sorrow or righteous anger. See Genesis 37:29,34; 44:13; Numbers 14:6; Joshua 7:6; and 2 Samuel 1:11–12.) Blasphemy was to be punished by death (Matthew 26:66; Leviticus 24:16). For that, Jesus is now taken to Pilate.

Discussing the Text

1. Suppose that you were John, one of Jesus' disciples, observing the five questionings of Jesus from a distance or hearing about them. What might you have been feeling after each hearing?

2. Much that took place in the trial before Caiaphas was a farce. Yet the trial continued, and the Sanhedrin issued a conviction. How could this happen?

3. What were the two purposes of the hearing before Caiaphas?

4. Why did Jesus' responses anger Caiaphas?

5. What was Caiaphas' verdict? What was the punishment for Caiaphas' verdict?

6. Why was Jesus taken to Pilate?

Apply

It is easy—too easy—for us to see the wickedness of those who so abused justice to condemn Jesus. Perhaps it will be useful, then, to consider ourselves standing before Jesus when He judges the world someday. Plenty of *true* witnesses could be called to condemn us to eternal death! All of our sins are in reality disrespect, abuse, and injustices against Jesus.

Immediately, however, we may again reverse roles, reminding ourselves that Jesus stood before the judge in our place. He willingly accepted every charge, each of which really should have been against us. He accepted the death penalty that we deserved so that we can be set free. Scripture often speaks of our salvation and forgiveness in courtroom terms (Daniel 7:9–14; Romans 8:33–34; Galatians 2:16; 1 John 2:1), and this story can help us visualize that concept. Jesus on trial and condemned to death means we need never face an angry Judge. In Him we are declared "Not guilty!"

1. Why is it important for us to see ourselves as those who condemned Jesus to death?

2. What does it mean to us that Jesus stood before the judge *in our place*?

3. Why is it important for us to realize that every charge against us for our sin was a charge Jesus accepted on our behalf?

4. How do Jesus' trial, condemnation, and death provide us comfort and hope?

30

5. In 15 words or less, summarize the truth revealed in Isaiah 53:4–6; Romans 4:25–5:1; 1 Corinthians 15:3; Hebrews 9:28; and 1 Peter 2:24–25.

6. Why do you think Scripture repeats this truth so often?

Catechism Connection

Examine the Eighth Commandment and Luther's explanation in the opening for this session.

1. How did the witness before the Sanhedrin (Matthew 26:59–61) break the Eighth Commandment?

2. Read 1 Samuel 19:4–6. How did God bless Jonathan's efforts to obey the Eighth Commandment?

3. What key to keeping the Eighth Commandment do you find in 1 Corinthians 13:7?

Send

To Do This Week

Family Connection

1. Review with your family the events of Jesus' last night and day before His crucifixion.

2. Discuss how our sins caused Jesus to withstand injustice and ridicule.

3. Describe how Jesus might have felt as He stood before the religious leaders of His day.

4. Give thanks to God for the forgiveness of sins and eternal life Jesus won for us by His suffering and death on the cross.

For Personal Reflection

1. Reread Matthew 26:57–66. Put yourself into the events of that night. How would you have responded to the charges brought against Jesus?

2. Meditate on the horror Jesus experienced as He willingly endured ridicule and considered His suffering and death.

3. Share with a friend or loved one the great love that God has demonstrated through His Son's death on the cross.

For Next Week

Read Matthew 28:1–10; John 20:1–18; Acts 10:34–43; and Colossians 3:1–4 in preparation for the next session.

Session 4

Jesus Rises from the Dead

(Matthew 28:1–10; John 20:1–18;
Acts 10:34–43; Colossians 3:1–4)

Gather

Theme: Do Not Be Afraid!

Key Point

Through His resurrection from the dead, Jesus demonstrated His victory for us over death. Because He lives, we shall also live.

Objectives

By the power of the Holy Spirit working through God's Word, we will
1. describe the events of the resurrection;
2. explain the significance of the events of the resurrection for our lives; and
3. share the peace that Jesus' resurrection from the dead provides us.

Opening

Sing or speak together the first two stanzas of "I Know That My Redeemer Lives."

I know that my Redeemer lives!
What comfort this sweet sentence gives!
He lives, He lives, who once was dead;
He lives, my ever-living head!

He lives triumphant from the grave;
He lives eternally to save;
He lives exalted, throned above;
He lives to rule His Church in love.

Introduction

1. What do you fear most?

2. Surveys have indicated that people fear death more than any other thing. Give evidence of this fear.

3. Why and how can Christians lay aside this fear?

Today, we will examine the central message of the resurrection—"Do not be afraid! He is risen!"—and its significance to all who believe in Jesus as Savior.

Study

Read aloud or skim Matthew 28:1–10; John 20:1–18; Acts 10:34–43; and Colossians 3:1–4.

Reading the Text

"The third day He rose again from the dead." The Christian church lives by that confession. "If Christ has not been raised, your faith is futile; you are still in your sins" (1 Corinthians 15:17). And if Christ had not returned from death, those disciples who had abandoned Him and fled could never have become the courageous missionaries who witnessed to the Gospel at the cost of their lives. Appropriately, then, three sessions, beginning this week, will focus on the events of Easter.

By Hebrew counting, the "third day" had arrived. On Friday afternoon, Jesus had been laid in the tomb of Joseph of Arimathea (Matthew 27:57–61). Since the Jewish people counted days beginning with the current one, that had been day one. From sundown

Friday until sunset Saturday (the Sabbath), Christ's body had remained lifeless. That had been day two, since the Jews considered evening to be the beginning of a new day. Now the sun had set on Saturday. Day three had begun.

The first events of that third day quite escaped human notice, and not only because they took place through the night. Outside Jesus' sealed tomb, guards kept watch in the darkness. But suddenly inside the tomb, the soul of Jesus—which since the moment of His death had been in Paradise—was reunited with His body. Jesus was alive again! His first act was likewise invisible to the world: with the tomb still closed, Jesus immediately descended into hell, not to suffer further but to announce His victory to Satan and the lost souls already there (1 Peter 3:18–19).

Meanwhile, the souls on earth sensed nothing significant. Through the same night, beginning as soon as the Sabbath had ended at sunset, women who had followed Jesus prepared spices—myrrh and aloes—to perfume a body they fully expected to decay. Clearly Jesus' friends had missed His several promises of resurrection (Matthew 16:21; 17:9, 23; 20:19), although they may still have hoped for a return by Christ at the end of the world. (Ironically, the guards had been posted specifically because Christ's enemies *did* know His prophecies. See Matthew 27:62–64.)

Christ's resurrection became evident when an angel descended with an earthquake and rolled away the large, flat stone that had closed the tomb (Matthew 28:2). Such a stone, shaped like a coin standing on its edge, would be fitted into a groove in the ground that ran downhill into a depression in front of the entrance. To reopen the tomb, therefore, required rolling the heavy stone uphill out of the depression—a very difficult task (Mark 16:3–4).

It was still dark when the women set out for the tomb (John 20:1) and first dawn as they arrived (Mark 14:2). At least five women came, perhaps in more than one group: Mary Magdalene (Matthew 28:1; Luke 8:2), the "other Mary" (who was probably the mother of Jesus' disciple known as James the Less, the wife of Clopas, and the sister of Jesus' mother, Mark 15:40; 16:1; John 19:25), Salome (probably James and John's mother; Mark 16:1; Matthew 27:56), Joanna (Luke 24:10; Luke 8:3), and at least one other (Luke 24:10).

It seems most likely that Mary Magdalene, seeing the stone rolled away, went no closer, but turned and ran back to tell Peter and John (John 20:1–2). Those women who did approach were met by angels, one sitting on the stone outside the tomb (Matthew 28:2) and perhaps two others inside (Luke 24:2–4). The angels' message expresses the same primary emphases in each account: (1) Jesus truly is risen, as evidenced by the obvious fact that He is not here where they laid Him (Matthew 28:6; Mark 16:6b; Luke 24:6a). (2) Jesus' resurrection is precisely according to His word (Matthew 28:6; Mark 16:7; Luke 24:6b–8). (3) Because Jesus is risen, there is no longer any need to be afraid (Matthew 28:4–5; 28:8–10; Mark 16:5–6; and Luke 24:5). (4) The witnesses of Christ's resurrection now have something important to tell (Matthew 28:7, 8–10; also Mark 16:7; and Luke 24:9). Matthew particularly emphasizes the need to go and tell.

John's gospel, which records few of the angels' words, conveys the same four emphases in other ways (John 20:1–18). Presumably after leaving the other women at the tomb, certainly before looking inside or seeing an angel, Mary Magdalene runs back to tell Peter and John what she assumes has happened: someone has moved His body, most likely to desecrate it or at least to prevent the site from becoming a martyr's monument. Hurrying to the tomb, the disciples do not see an angel, but they receive equally powerful evidence that Jesus is alive: the empty tomb is not the work of grave robbers, who would have worked roughly and in haste; the grave cloth is neatly, patiently folded (John 20:3–7). That is evidence enough for John. He believes that Jesus is alive. Later, though, he will also realize that Scripture had already presented sufficient proof, for all this was exactly as promised (20:8–9).

Unlike the other women, Mary Magdalene does not tremble with fear at the appearance of the angels. In fact, they apparently veil their radiance so that she sees in them nothing out of the ordinary (John 20:11–13). But Mary has deep fears of her own—the thought of her Lord's body being abused is more than she can bear—and Jesus allays those fears with one gentle word: her name (20:14–16). (Jesus, too, may have used His power to conceal His identity, as He did in Luke 24:15–16. Alternatively, Mary's tears and grief that so turned her attention inward may have prevented her from recognizing Him.)

Now Mary also receives the instruction to go and tell (John 20:17–18). This was probably the point of Jesus' command that she not hold on to Him. Certainly she could touch Him, but she was to get on with her new mission, not cling to Him.

Discussing the Text

1. Compare Matthew's account of the resurrection to John's.

2. The Apostles' Creed says, "The third day He rose again from the dead." How can this be true if Jesus died on a Friday and rose on Sunday?

3. The angels' message in Matthew's gospel and the events in the account included in John's gospel emphasize what four facts?

4. What significance do we find in the words of the angel and the words of Jesus in Matthew 28:7 and 10 and in John 20:17?

5. Read Acts 10:39–43. How did Peter explain the reason Jesus appeared to people after His resurrection?

Apply

As Jesus' crucifixion finished His mission to save the human race (John 19:30), His resurrection proved His work of redemption had been completed. The significance of Jesus' resurrection, then, can best be described by what it proves.

First, Jesus' rising from the dead proves that He is the Son of God (Romans 1:4). Under oath, Jesus had claimed to be God's Son. Had He been an impostor, the heavenly Father would never have let Him rise from the dead.

Second, the resurrection proves that everything else Jesus said is true (Luke 24:6–8). To say He would rise again was the most difficult promise Jesus had ever made. Since He kept this one, we can be sure He will keep every promise He has made to us.

Third, Jesus' resurrection demonstrates that God the Father has accepted Christ's death as a sufficient sacrifice for the sins of the world. God had poured out His anger on His Son, but now, in raising Jesus, He shows that He is no longer angry. God is satisfied; we are forgiven.

Finally, the resurrection of Christ proves that we will rise someday, too. Because He lives, we shall live also (John 14:19).

All this means that we need never fear anything. Jesus' promises to care for us are trustworthy. God the Father is watching over us as a loving Father indeed. Even death cannot hurt us. "Do not be afraid! He is risen!"

1. Jesus' crucifixion finished His mission. What was the purpose of Jesus' resurrection from the dead?

2. Examine the four things above that Jesus' resurrection proved. How might you respond to people who claim some or all of these things are unbelievable?

3. What does Jesus' resurrection mean to you?

4. What are some traditions that help make Easter meaningful to your family?

Catechism Connection

Examine the Second Article and Luther's explanation in the opening for Session 1.

1. Read Colossians 3:1–10. What does Paul say about a believer's position in Christ in verse 3a? 1a? 9b?

2. What directives does Paul give as a result of our position in Christ in verse 2? 5? 8?

3. Summarize what Paul says to believers in these verses.

Send

To Do This Week

Family Connection

1. Review the events of the resurrection with your family.

2. Have each person in your family share what Jesus' resurrection means to them.

3. Design, write, and send Easter cards to your friends and loved ones that tell of the significance of the resurrection for your lives.

For Personal Reflection

1. Write in your own words a prayer thanking Jesus for the meaning the resurrection provides for your life.

2. Tell a friend or loved one this week, "Do not be afraid!" Share the reason that you do not fear death.

3. Pray that the Holy Spirit would enable you to share Easter joy with others every day of your life.

For Next Week

Read John 20:19–31; Acts 2:14–41; 4:1–31; and 1 Peter 1:3–9 in preparation for the next session.

Session 5

We Know That Jesus Rose from the Dead

(John 20:19–31; Acts 2:14–41; 4:1–31; 1 Peter 1:3–9)

Gather

Theme: Peace

Key Point

Jesus' resurrection provides proof that Jesus' sacrifice for our sins was accepted by God. We can live with the peace that passes all understanding, for God assures us in His Word that our sins are forgiven and we will live eternally with Him in heaven.

Objectives

By the power of the Holy Spirit working through God's Word, we will

1. describe the events immediately following the resurrection;
2. explain the significance of each of the resurrection events for Jesus' disciples—and for us; and
3. share with others the peace God provides through His Son's resurrection.

Opening

Speak together "Christ Is Arisen."
  Christ is arisen
  From the grave's dark prison.
  So let our song exulting rise:
  Christ with comfort lights our eyes.
  Alleluia!

All our hopes were ended
Had Jesus not ascended
From the grave triumphantly
Our never-ending life to be.
Alleluia!
So let our song exulting rise:
Christ, our comfort, fills the skies.
Alleluia!

Introduction

1. What words or phrases come to mind when you think of the concept of peace?

2. Underline the words or phrases that describe peace as the world would explain it.

3. Circle those words or phrases that describe peace as only God can provide it.

4. How is the world's view of peace different than the peace God provides by His grace through faith in the resurrected Jesus?

In today's session we will learn of the peace that only God can and does provide through His Son's life, death, and resurrection—a peace that passes all human understanding.

Study

Read aloud John 20:19–31; Acts 2:14–41; 4:1–31; and 1 Peter 1:3–9.

Reading the Text

Jesus was risen. Death had been conquered. Still, for anyone to benefit from Jesus' resurrection, it had to be known, believed, and proclaimed. Making His resurrection known, therefore, was Jesus' next task, and it has become the task of the church ever since.

The evening of the first Easter Sunday finds the disciples gathered together, probably in the same large, upstairs room in which they had celebrated the Lord's Supper only three days before. Ten of the Twelve are there; Judas has committed suicide, and Thomas is absent for some reason. Other followers are present as well (Luke 24:33). By now, they have heard the reports of Mary Magdalene and the other women who have seen Jesus (John 20:18; Matthew 28:8–10), and at least John is convinced of the resurrection (John 20:8). Still, they have the door locked in fear (John 20:19), perhaps for that very reason; news of the empty tomb might drive the Jewish leaders to come looking for revenge. Moreover, the disciples are at a loss about what Jesus' rising might mean for them. It seems that whatever hope they had at this point, most of them could at best imagine Jesus' spirit, not His body, alive. That left them wondering what to do next.

Suddenly Jesus is among them (John 20:19). In His state of humiliation—His earlier time on earth—He did not use all of His divine powers. Now in His state of exaltation, the walls, doors, and locks present no barrier. His first words are the most comforting the disciples could hear: "Peace be with you!" Peace (*shalom* in Hebrew) meant the condition of total well-being that people could enjoy when, and only when, they were in a whole relationship with God. That, in turn, was possible only when sin, which makes humans enemies of God, was forgiven. Since the disciples had so recently deserted and denied Jesus, they actually had reason to be afraid of Him! They needed this assurance that He was not angry, but that they were instead reconciled with God and forgiven.

Next Jesus shows them that He is not just a spirit. He is fully human with the same body they had seen so often (John 20:20; Luke 24:37–40). He is even capable of eating (Luke 24:41–43). This is an

43

important understanding of the resurrection: not just our souls, but also our very same bodies will live forever in heaven. Of course, like Jesus' body, ours will be changed, or glorified (Philippians 3:20–21).

Finally Jesus commissions the disciples to go and share the peace of His resurrection with the world (John 20:21–23). All four gospels have accounts of Jesus sending out His apostles (see Matthew 28:19–20; Mark 16:15; Luke 24:46–49.) Specifically, the mission is to forgive sins. Forgiveness is integral to the Christian faith. When the apostles forgive or retain sins, it will be as if Jesus Himself were speaking.

Thomas' reaction after learning of this meeting is well known (John 20:24–25). He was not, however, always a "doubting Thomas." On other occasions he was willing to die with Jesus (John 11:5–8, 16) and eager to learn from Christ (John 14:1–6). After his doubts were resolved, a very strong faith drove him to spread the Gospel, possibly to India.

Seven days later, again on Sunday, Jesus returns (John 20:26–29). (After Easter, Jesus was no longer constantly seen in person with His disciples, but appeared to them on many occasions over the next 40 days. See Acts 1:3.) This time He comes especially for Thomas. Although He admonishes Thomas for his unbelief, Jesus extends to him the same "Peace be with you!" with which He had comforted the others. Jesus cares very deeply for Thomas.

The clear visual evidence Thomas had requested (John 20:25, 27) brings forth one of the clearest confessions of faith in the entire Bible: "My Lord and my God!" (John 20:28). It was crucial that all of the apostles see Jesus with their own eyes. Being an eyewitness to the resurrected Christ was a primary requirement for apostleship (Acts 1:21–22), since they were to be His first witnesses to the world.

Nevertheless, "blessed are those who have not seen and yet have believed" (John 20:29). All these centuries later, God still provides powerful evidence of Jesus' resurrection. The most important evidence is the testimony of Scripture itself. The very purpose of the Bible, John writes, is to bring about faith (and thereby salvation) in Jesus (John 20:30–31). As Scripture is read or heard, the Holy Spirit convinces that it is true, that Jesus is risen.

Other evidence is persuasive, too. The biblical accounts of Christ's resurrection have a solid historical foundation. For example, more eyewitnesses (certainly Matthew, Mark, John, Peter,

Paul, and James, and possibly Luke and Jude) have recorded their personal testimonies than those of virtually any other ancient event have. Paul even opened himself up to be verified or disproved by reminding people that the more than 500 witnesses of the resurrected Lord were still alive (1 Corinthians 15:6). Obviously, he was confident that he could not be disproved.

Even Jesus' enemies provide evidence of His rising. Some writers of the second century A.D. continued to report that the disciples had stolen Christ's body from the tomb. This verifies that the grave was indeed empty.

Yet one more proof of Jesus' resurrection must be considered. From cowering deserters, Christ's disciples became fearless preachers of the faith. On the day of Pentecost, Peter, with the others, was emboldened to proclaim to the same crowd that had crucified Jesus, "You … put Him to death … but God raised Him" (Acts 2:23–24). Most of the apostles were ultimately murdered for their convictions. Surely they would not have gone to their deaths for something that was fraudulent or at all uncertain. The disciples had no doubt. They *knew* Jesus was risen.

Discussing the Text

1. Examine Peter's words in Acts 2:22–25, 36 and in 1 Peter 1:3–9. What important truth related to Jesus' resurrection is evident in these words?

2. Compare Philippians 4:7 with John 20:19–21a. Why is the message of peace so important in both instances?

3. All four gospel accounts have Jesus sending out His apostles. What was their mission? What was the significance of their mission?

4. How does the resurrection of Jesus have a solid historical foundation? Why is this important?

5. Compare Matthew 26:56, John 20:19a, and Acts 4:13. Describe the change that took place in the disciples.

Apply

The accounts in this session suggest many important applications. Most significantly, of course, is the certainty that Jesus is truly living. We are strengthened as we hear, "Christ is risen!"

Further, we can learn to see Christ for ourselves as the One who personally absolves our sins. Because Jesus commissioned the apostles to forgive, even today when we hear forgiveness proclaimed and announced during worship, we can know Jesus Himself speaks. We can be certain that we are indeed forgiven.

Moreover, we have comfort in hearing that Jesus is patient with doubters. All of us will at some time struggle with questions and doubts about our faith. As Jesus dealt gently with Thomas, so He is patient with us.

Jesus' appearance on Easter evening also gives some of the most helpful hints as to the nature of our bodies in the resurrection. It is reassuring for us to know that in heaven we will still be ourselves—fully human, real and physical, with the same bodies we now have, but glorified.

Finally, we realize that we can witness to others about our faith in order to draw them to believe in Christ. The faith of Peter and the other apostles—for which they were willing to die—convinced many that Jesus really was the risen Savior. With us, too, faith "proved genuine" through "all kinds of trials" may help others who have not seen Jesus to be blessed by believing (1 Peter 1:3–9).

1. What comfort do you receive in hearing, "Christ is risen!"? See also Acts 17:2–4.

2. How does Jesus' commissioning of the apostles to forgive sins (John 20:21–23) continue to be lived out in the church today?

3. How does Jesus' patience with Thomas provide us comfort and hope? How might it provide others with comfort and hope?

4. What knowledge does Jesus' appearance to the disciples provide us about our bodies when we are resurrected from the dead on Judgment Day? See also Job 19:26 and 1 John 3:2.

5. How might opportunities to face trials provide us the chance to witness boldly about our faith in Jesus? See 1 Peter 3:15.

6. Discuss the significance of John 20:30–31.

Catechism Connection

Examine the Second Article and Luther's explanation in the opening for Session 1.

1. What do Luther's words "that I may be His own and live under Him in His kingdom and serve Him in everlasting righteousness, innocence, and blessedness," mean to you?

2. What additional insights do you find in Ephesians 2:8–10?

3. Read Romans 6:6–8. Why are we able to serve God?

Send

To Do This Week

Family Connection

1. Take time to review with your family the events of the resurrection and the response of the early church to Jesus' command to "go and tell."

2. How might you as a family "go and tell"?

3. Tell one another the meaning Jesus' resurrection has for your life and for your physical death.

4. Draw a family picture or poster of Jesus speaking the words "Peace be with you!" Include each of your family members in the picture.

For Personal Reflection

1. Consider how Jesus' words "Peace be with you!" remain important to you today.

2. Consider how at times you are like Thomas. Confess your sinfulness to Jesus with the assurance that Jesus graciously forgives all who come to Him.

3. Share the message of the resurrection with a friend or loved one who seems to have little peace in his or her life.

For Next Week

Read Luke 24:13–35 in preparation for the next session.

Session 6

Jesus Appears to Two Disciples

(Luke 24:13–35)

Gather

Theme: An Eyewitness

Key Point

Through eyewitness accounts of Jesus' victory over sin, death, and the power of the devil, God empowers us to witness to others of His life, death, and resurrection.

Objectives

By the power of the Holy Spirit working through God's Word, we will

1. recount the events of Jesus' appearance to the disciples on the road to Emmaus;
2. describe how Scripture makes us eyewitnesses of God's love revealed in the person and work of Jesus; and
3. witness boldly what God has revealed to us in Scripture.

Opening

Read the following portions of Martin Luther's explanations of the Lord's Supper responsively.

Leader: What is the Sacrament of the Altar?

Participants: It is the true body and blood of our Lord Jesus Christ under the bread and wine, instituted by Christ Himself for us Christians to eat and to drink.

Leader: What is the benefit of this eating and drinking?

Participants: These words, "Given and shed for you for the forgiveness of sins," show us that in the Sacrament forgiveness of sins, life, and salvation are given us through these words. For where there is forgiveness of sins, there is also life and salvation.

Leader: How can bodily eating and drinking do such great things?

Participants: Certainly not just eating and drinking do these things, but the words written here: "Given and shed for you for the forgiveness of sins." These words, along with the bodily eating and drinking, are the main thing in the Sacrament. Whoever believes these words has exactly what they say: "forgiveness of sins."

Introduction

1. What is the importance of an eyewitness account of an event?

2. Why are eyewitness accounts of the resurrection of Jesus important?

3. As a student of Scripture, how are you an eyewitness of Jesus' resurrection?

In today's session, as we review eyewitness accounts of the resurrection, we will come to realize how God through His Word has made us eyewitnesses of His love and mercy demonstrated in the person and work of Jesus.

Study

Read Luke 24:13–35.

Reading the Text

The appearance of Jesus on the road to Emmaus is among the most vivid, detailed post-resurrection reports of the four gospels. As we read the text, we are, in one respect, eyewitnesses to the resurrection. The emphasis in this story, though, is that the *written* word delivers all one needs to know of Christ's mission accomplished.

It is still Easter, earlier, in fact, than Jesus' first appearance to the Twelve. Two disciples—not of the Twelve but of the larger group—leave Jerusalem for Emmaus, a town at the end of a lovely valley some seven miles to the northwest (Luke 24:13). One of them is named Cleopas (Luke 24:18).

Like the disciples back in Jerusalem, these two are struggling to make sense of the past days' events. They, too, have heard the reports of Jesus' resurrection—probably not only the "vision of angels" seen by the women and the empty tomb witnessed by Peter and John, but also Christ's conversations with Mary Magdalene and the other women. Were the women imagining things? Or was it simply Jesus' spirit they saw? They wonder. It is all very unsatisfying.

The road takes them up over a rocky plateau. Perhaps as they enter the valley, still climbing gently toward Emmaus, a stranger joins in their walk (Luke 24:15–16). It is, literally, a miracle that they do not recognize Jesus. He prevents them from knowing Him because He wants to teach them where they may discover Him without seeing.

Jesus' question stops them in their tracks: "What are you discussing together as you walk along?" We can imagine a long silence. They turn to look Him in the eye, then drop their heads and draw a slow, deep breath at the prospect of telling the whole, sad story. How could this stranger have been in Jerusalem and not known? All the people had known Jesus of Nazareth to be a mighty prophet. They hate to even think about it now. Rumors of some sort of vision or spiritual visitation by Jesus are no consolation; to redeem Israel (that is, to drive out the Romans, as they had hoped) would require a real, physical, earthly leader, not some spirit. They can see nothing good coming of this tragedy.

Perhaps for a moment they are offended when the stranger seems so at ease with their tragedy, when He actually upbraids them as "foolish" and "slow of heart to believe all that the prophets have spoken" (24:25). Immediately He begins to explain what those prophets had always meant (24:26–27). *The entire Old Testament demonstrates that the Messiah had to suffer death and then be raised in glory.* ("Moses and all the Prophets" was a common expression for the whole Hebrew Bible.) The events of the last few days had been no setback for God's plans. In fact, the disciples should have expected them. The moving Bible class probably lasts between one and two hours. All the while, as the disciples realize later, their "hearts were burning within" (24:32).

Finally they reach Emmaus. They long for this welcome stranger to stay with them (24:28–29). (The beloved hymn "Abide with Me" is based on this text.) He obliges, then again surprises: as the evening meal is served, the guest suddenly becomes the host, taking, blessing, and breaking the bread (24:30–31). At last they recognize Him! They have seen Him do this before! The breaking of bread is a reminder of the Lord's Supper, in which Jesus will continue to be really present with His church. The disciples themselves later emphasize that they recognized Christ's presence in this act (24:35).

Instantly Jesus is gone, but the disciples are no longer sad. They must return to the city and tell their friends—even if it means stumbling the last steps in the dark. This time they must have run the distance (24:33).

The disciples in Jerusalem are just as eager to see them, for they have news of their own: Jesus is alive! Some time during the afternoon He had also appeared to Peter (Luke 24:34). The Savior's promises were indeed all true!

Discussing the Text

1. Why did Jesus prevent the disciples on the road to Emmaus from recognizing Him?

2. Discuss the significance of Luke 24:27.

3. How had the events the disciples contemplated fulfilled rather than set back God's plans?

4. Of what would the breaking of the bread remind the disciples?

5. How were the disciples eyewitnesses of Jesus' resurrection? How did Jesus reveal the truth concerning His resurrection to the disciples? Why was this important?

6. Discuss the pattern of Christian ministry displayed by the two disciples when they returned "at once" (verse 33) to Jerusalem.

Apply

Jesus calls us to believe in Him without seeing. The story of the walk to Emmaus elaborates the truth that Jesus comes to His disciples in the Scriptures. The Bible gives us the full revelation to know Jesus personally and intimately.

The key to the Scriptures, meanwhile, is Jesus Himself. Every word of the Bible, Old and New Testament, points to Christ. The Bible is not primarily a manual, a collection of how-tos for happy living, but rather it is the story of God saving us in Christ. Each passage either shows us our need for Christ (the Law) or declares or applies what He has done to meet that need (the Gospel). Learning to look for Christ on every page of Scripture is a most precious lifelong skill.

1. How does Scripture make us eyewitnesses of Jesus' resurrection?

2. How is Jesus the key to understanding Scripture? See John 5:39 and Galatians 1:3–4.

3. Why would looking for Christ on every page of Scripture be a precious lifelong skill? What opportunities do you have to follow the example of the Bereans (Acts 17:11)?

Catechism Connection

Examine the portions of Luther's explanations of the Lord's Supper included in the opening for this session.

1. How do we know that we receive Christ's body and blood in the Sacrament—that Christ's words are not picture language? See 1 Corinthians 10:16 and 11:23–29.

2. Why may we not say that the body and blood of Christ in the Sacrament are sacrificed again to God for the sins of the living and the dead? See Hebrews 10:14, 18.

3. Read 1 Peter 2:24. Describe the strength we receive in the Sacrament.

Send

To Do This Week

Family Connection

1. Review all of the Easter accounts. Ask each family member to tell one event that is particularly meaningful to them.

2. Ask, "Why is it important that we study Scripture regularly?" Remind your family that every word of the Bible points to Jesus. Then say, "In order for us to know Jesus, we study God's Word regularly." Develop a plan where your family can spend some time each week studying God's Word.

3. Reenact the story of the disciples on the road to Emmaus. Take turns pretending that you are the disciples. After acting out the story ask, "To whom could we run to tell about the risen Jesus?" List names of people whom you will tell of God's love in Jesus this week.

For Personal Reflection

1. Review the Easter accounts from each of the gospels. How are they different? Similar? How does each gospel account give additional information concerning the resurrection?

2. Set aside time each day to study God's Word. Look for God's Law and God's Gospel in every passage.

3. Consider the enthusiasm the disciples must have had as they left Emmaus and returned to Jerusalem to tell others what they had seen. You too have witnessed the power of God's love in Christ in your life. How do you demonstrate your enthusiasm for all that God has done for you?

For Next Week

Read Acts 6:1–8:1 in preparation for the next session.

Session 7

Stephen Tells about Jesus

(Acts 6:1–8:1)

Gather

Theme: A Martyr!

Key Point

God's love for us enables us to face persecution, rejection, or disapproval, confident that He is with us, will deliver us, and ultimately will use the experience as an opportunity to strengthen our faith.

Objectives

By the power of the Holy Spirit working through God's Word, we will

1. list details of Stephen's message;
2. describe evidence of Stephen's faith even as he faced certain death; and
3. remain faithful even as we face persecution, rejection, or disapproval, confident of Jesus' presence in our lives.

Opening

Read the Fifth Petition of the Lord's Prayer and Martin Luther's explanation responsively.

All: And forgive us our trespasses as we forgive those who trespass against us.

Leader: What does this mean?

Group 1: We pray in this petition that our Father in heaven would not look at our sins, or deny our prayer because of them.

Group 2: We are neither worthy of the things for which we pray, nor have we deserved them, but we ask that He would give them all to us by grace, for we daily sin much and surely deserve nothing but punishment.

All: So we too will sincerely forgive and gladly do good to those who sin against us.

Introduction

1. Have you or someone you know faced persecution, rejection, or disapproval because of the Christian faith? Describe the event.

2. What was the result?

In today's session we learn of the first Christian martyr. We will focus not so much on Stephen, but instead on the power of God's Spirit working through Stephen, which enabled Stephen to witness boldly about his faith even as he faced death. God gives to His people today the same power evident in the life of Stephen. He strengthens our faith by the power of the Holy Spirit working through Word and Sacrament.

Study

Read aloud Acts 6:1–8:1.

Reading the Text

After His resurrection, Jesus sent His disciples out to be His witnesses to the world. What a glorious calling! But the history of the church has shown that testifying about Christ also has a cost. The Greek word for *witness* is the same word from which we get *martyr*. To be a follower of Jesus means to follow Him *everywhere* He went—to heaven, certainly, but also, first, to the cross

(Matthew 16:24). In today's session, Stephen becomes the first Christian to witness about Christ at the cost of his life.

Ironically, Stephen's martyrdom took place during the prospering of the young church. Still only a brief time after Jesus' return to heaven and Pentecost, the church has been growing rapidly (Acts 2:41; 4:4; 5:14; 6:7), now numbering at least 5,000. While nearly all are Jews and in Jerusalem, they are of two backgrounds: native Hebrews (from Palestine and Aramaic-speaking) and Hellenistic Jews (originally from other lands and primarily Greek-speaking).

The believers have been enjoying a unity of heart and mind, gathering every day for meals and sharing their possessions with any in need (2:44–46; 4:32–35). At this point, the apostles themselves still handle the task of distributing food to the huge congregation. But this cannot continue. Others could manage this responsibility just as ably, and it demands time that the apostles ought to devote to preaching and prayer. When a misunderstanding arises between the Hebrews and the Hellenists, they wisely establish a new order (Acts 6:1–6).

The seven men chosen for the task are all of good reputation, full of the Holy Spirit, and possessing sound judgment. All have Greek names, suggesting that special care was given to those Hellenistic widows who might have been disadvantaged. Of the men listed in this passage, we know more only about Philip (8:5–8, 26–40; 21:8) and Stephen.

The mission of these seven men was purely to administer temporal matters of the church; they were not ordained into the "ministry of the word" (6:4). Nevertheless, the Spirit enabled Stephen both to perform miracles and to proclaim Christ with power. (Every Christian, of course, is to witness for Christ outside the public worship service.) So effective was Stephen that some opponents from one of the synagogues became jealous and concocted charges to bring him before the Sanhedrin (6:8–12). Perhaps Saul knew some of Stephen's disputers and became especially interested in the case.

The Sanhedrin was the same council that had condemned Jesus to die, probably headed again by Caiaphas. Again false witnesses were called, and the charges were similar (Acts 6:13–14; Matthew 26:59–61). As with Jesus, there was a serenity about Stephen that everyone could see (Acts 6:15).

Unlike Jesus, however, Stephen offers a lengthy defense (Acts 7:2–53). Although he is not allowed to finish, the point of Stephen's speech becomes progressively clear: the religious leaders have repeated history; they have killed the Righteous One just as their forefathers resisted God and His representatives time and again.

To make his point, Stephen recounts the long history of Israel, beginning with Abraham. He condenses many incidents into a few sentences, but he also adds certain details not given in the Old Testament. For example, Abraham, Stephen explains, was called by God while still in his first home, Ur of the Chaldeans in Mesopotamia, not at his intermediate stop, Haran, as the Genesis account might seem to imply (compare Acts 7:2–4 with Genesis 11:31–12:5). Not only Joseph, but the other patriarchs of the twelve tribes of Israel were buried in Canaan, not Egypt (Acts 7:16; Genesis 50:22–25; Joshua 24:32). And to the story of Moses (Exodus 2:1–15), Stephen adds Moses' rich education in Egypt (Acts 7:22) and the fact that Moses intended his rash killing of an Egyptian to begin to deliver Israel from slavery (Acts 7:25).

This last statement is more than incidental. Stephen blames the Israelites, for they failed to realize that God was rescuing them through Moses. And that message recurs through Stephen's entire speech, becoming more biting with each illustration. Joseph had been sold by his brothers, the fathers of the nation (Acts 7:9; Genesis 37:18–28). Moses was rejected by Israel, though he was sent by God (Acts 7:35), and the people instead turned to idolatry (7:39–42; Exodus 32:1–4). They had, in fact, persecuted one prophet after another. And although God had given them circumcision as a sign of His grace (Acts 7:8), they remained to this day people with "uncircumcised hearts and ears," who "always resist the Holy Spirit," just as their fathers had (Acts 7:51).

Meanwhile, Stephen reminds, God had throughout the Old Testament given signs of His coming to dwell with His people. An "angel" had accompanied Moses (Acts 7:35, 38); the "angel of the Lord" in the Old Testament is often the Son of God. Moses had promised that God would send another prophet, the Messiah (Acts 7:37; Deuteronomy 18:15). Even the tabernacle and the temple, which Stephen was accused of denigrating, were not significant in themselves (Acts 7:48–50), but only symbols of God coming to live on earth.

Now the climax: just as Israel had constantly rejected God's spokesmen, this generation had now betrayed and killed that One to whom Moses, the temple, and all the Old Testament had pointed: "the Righteous One." Everyone present knows that Stephen is speaking of Jesus, whom they had murdered. As the last straw, Stephen declares the same vision that brought cries of blasphemy against Jesus: the Son of Man at the right hand of God.

The council will not hear another word (Acts 7:57). At Jesus' trial they feigned the formality of a verdict. Here there is none. This is a mob lynching (Acts 7:58).

Yet, as is true of every Christian martyr, Stephen shares in the death of Christ. He recalls the words of Jesus on the cross: "Lord Jesus, receive my spirit" (Acts 7:59; Luke 23:46) and, finally, "Lord, do not hold this sin against them" (Acts 7:60; Luke 23:34).

Discussing the Text

1. Read Acts 6:1–6. What misunderstanding occurred between the Hellenist and Hebrew Jews? What did the early church do to rectify the situation?

2. What was the reason for charges brought against Stephen (6:8–12)?

3. How was Stephen's trial similar to Jesus' trial before the Sanhedrin? How was it different?

4. Summarize Stephen's defense before the Sanhedrin.

5. Why might Stephen have begun his defense with a reference to Abraham (7:2; see also John 8:39 and Genesis 12:2–3)? How is that reference meaningful for us today, also?

6. Why do you think God caused the writer of Acts to include the lengthy answer that Stephen gave to the Sanhedrin (7:2–53)?

7. What caused the Sanhedrin to react violently? How did the Sanhedrin respond to Stephen's message?

8. What words of Jesus does Stephen recall as the council stones him?

Apply

The tragedy of Stephen's death may seem far removed from our day and country, but it may be closer to home than we initially think. The fact is, more Christians died for their faith in the 20th century than in the first 19 centuries combined. According to one current study, some 200 million Christians worldwide are living under persecution, and another 400 million face various forms of discrimination because of their faith. We need to pray for these brothers and sisters in Christ and to learn more about how we can help.

Further, we may be subjected to persecution of a subtler nature. It may be helpful to talk about pressure or ridicule we receive as believers in Christ. We may not realize, too, that the bombardment of sinful influences on television, in movies, and in popular music, and even on the Internet is a form of persecution against our desire to live a Christian lifestyle.

It is important to realize that enduring persecution as a Christian is to share in the sufferings of Christ (2 Corinthians 4:10). While persecution is always painful—physically, emotionally, or in other ways—it is also an experience for which we can actually give thanks (Acts 5:40–42). With persecution comes the promise of Christ's presence to deliver us. Persecution even serves to strengthen faith. Through the centuries, the church has thrived during times of persecution. It is often said that "the blood of the martyrs is the lifeblood of the church."

1. What subtle forms of persecution may we or other Christians experience?

2. How does enduring persecution share in the sufferings of Christ? See also Acts 5:41; Romans 8:17; and Philippians 3:10–11.

3. How can persecution actually serve to strengthen faith? See Romans 5:3–5.

4. Explain the statement "The blood of the martyrs is the lifeblood of the church."

5. What kind of suffering for your faith have you or your acquaintances experienced?

6. What blessings, if any, have come through this suffering?

Catechism Connection

Examine the Fifth Petition and Luther's explanation in the opening for this session.

1. Read Acts 5:29–32. How strongly did Peter emphasize forgiveness?

2. Read Colossians 3:1–2, 12–14. Where do we receive the power to forgive others?

3. Discuss the significance of forgiveness in family and congregational life.

Send

To Do This Week

Family Connection

1. Discuss the concept of martyrdom with your family.

2. Review the events of the story. Then ask, "How was God the real hero in this story?"

3. Have family members role-play forgiving one another. In the days that follow, look for opportunities to forgive or to ask for forgiveness.

4. Discuss how at times we are persecuted or rejected for our faith. Ask family members to share times when they have felt embarrassed or ridiculed because of their faith. Remind family members that the Holy Spirit working through God's Word will enable and empower them to witness boldly about faith in Christ Jesus even when doing so is unpopular.

For Personal Reflection

1. Consider some of the major issues in society, where scriptural truth has been rejected in order to compensate for people's feelings and attitudes; for example, abortion, euthanasia, and sexuality. How can you continue to share that which God desires in a hostile world?

2. Consider the last words of Stephen as the council stoned him: "Lord, do not hold this sin against them." How do these words demonstrate his faith in Christ Jesus? How might these words be appropriate for you to speak as you face persecution or rejection because of your faith?

3. Spend time daily studying God's Word. Pray that by the power of the Holy Spirit you may witness boldly to unbelievers about the love of God in Christ Jesus.

For Next Week

Read Acts 17:1–34 and 23:12–35 in preparation for the next session.

Session 8

Paul Proclaims the Gospel

(Acts 17:1–34; 23:12–35)

Gather

Theme: Empty

Key Point

Jesus came to earth to empty Himself, receiving the punishment we deserved because of sin (death on the cross), so that we might proclaim the blessings He provides—forgiveness of sin and life eternal.

Objectives

By the power of the Holy Spirit working through God's Word, we will
1. describe the way Paul tailored the message of the Gospel to meet people's needs;
2. summarize the message Paul shared; and
3. share with others the rich blessings that God has given us.

Opening

Read the First Commandment and Martin Luther's explanation responsively.

All: You shall have no other gods.

Leader: What does this mean?

Participants: We should fear, love, and trust in God above all things.

Introduction

"I feel empty inside."

1. What might cause you or someone you know to speak these words?

2. Many people today spend their lives seeking that which will fill the emptiness they experience. What are some things people do to fill the emptiness?

In today's session we will learn that all people who do not have faith in Jesus are empty and seek to fill that emptiness through many means. Ultimately, all those who are empty of faith in Jesus will face the same consequence—eternal death. But God equips His people to share His Law and His Gospel so that through their message others will be filled—filled with saving faith, filled with the forgiveness of sins, filled with the assurance of eternal life. St. Paul preached to people who were spiritually empty so that they might share in the victory Jesus won for them on the cross.

Study

Read aloud Acts 17:1–34 and 23:12–35.

Reading the Text

After the death of Stephen, one individual takes center stage for the remainder of the book of Acts. The story of Saul's conversion from a bitter enemy of the church to the great missionary we know as St. Paul is a remarkable part of early church history. Some years after becoming a believer, Paul, together with Barnabas, made Christianity's first recorded intentional mission expedition, establishing congregations in Cyprus and Asia Minor (Acts 13–14).

This week's lessons include a portion of Paul's second missionary journey. After first returning to strengthen the young churches in

Asia Minor, Paul and his new partner, Silas, have now been directed by the Holy Spirit to cross over into Europe (15:36–16:40), specifically Macedonia and then Greece.

Along the famous Roman road, the Egnation Way, is the largest city of ancient Macedonia: Thessalonica. As was his custom, Paul begins his work here by preaching in the Jewish synagogue (17:1–3). Using the Old Testament as his basis, Paul shows that Jesus in every way fits God's promises of the Messiah. Above all, the point of his message is Jesus' resurrection.

Tragically, while some of his fellow Jews believe, more become jealous when many God-fearing Gentiles, who followed the God of Israel but had never been circumcised, also receive the message (17:4–9). Some of the Jews are so bent on denouncing Paul that they deny even their own religion to gain the favor of city authorities; they profess undivided loyalty to the Roman emperor even though their hope has always been that God will send them another king.

From Thessalonica, Paul moves on to Berea, 50 miles to the southwest (Acts 17:10). What a noble example the Bereans are—carefully, daily searching the Scriptures to confirm Paul's words (17:11)!

Now perhaps the most famous of all Paul's visits: Athens. The chief city of Greece, Athens was also the cultural center of the entire empire, renowned for its sculpture, architecture, oratory, drama, and poetry. The Athenians were very "religious," worshiping the many gods and goddesses remembered in Greek mythology. The city had also been home to the great philosophers Socrates, Plato, and Aristotle. Yet it was morally bankrupt. Prostitution and homosexuality were accepted—indeed honored—parts of life. The two dominant philosophies of Paul's day, Stoicism and Epicureanism, both expressed the emptiness of paganism. Stoics resigned themselves to fate; Epicureans "lived it up" with pleasure, since they saw nothing else for which to live.

The marketplace, also called the agora, was the location of Paul's encounter with the Athenians (17:16–18). The professional philosophers were apparently not highly impressed with Paul; they called him, literally, "one who picks up scraps," that is, an amateur thinker who only borrows the ideas of others. In addition, they did not understand him; they believe he was proclaiming strange or foreign gods. But they are intrigued, for they invite him to address them formally at the Areopagus (17:19–21).

The Areopagus, or Mars Hill (named for Ares or Mars, the god of war), was the meeting place of the council that oversaw all religious and cultural affairs of Athens. The Areopagus was both the name of the council and the physical location where the council met. Paul's speech, therefore, is a classic moment—the Christian faith encountering the pride of pagan thought.

For the moment, Paul abandons his usual methods, employing instead the style of argumentation familiar to the Athenians. (This is Paul's one and only attempt at apologetics, the use of logic to argue for the existence of God.) He introduces his message with an illustration from the local paganism: so careful have the Athenians been not to offend any god that they have erected an idol TO AN UNKNOWN GOD. This God, Paul says, he will now declare to them (17:22–31).

Paul's God is more powerful than any of the Greek deities, for He made the world and all things (17:24). Greek mythology taught that the current gods and goddesses were themselves created, and each of them, even the chief god Zeus, had jurisdiction only over certain areas. Yet, such an almighty God surely did exist, for even some of the Athenians' own poets acknowledged that every person was the offspring of one Father (17:28).

After laying all this foundation in logic, Paul comes to his points, both Law and Gospel (17:30–31). The ignorance of the Athenians can continue no longer; it is now time to repent! But there is hope, for God's Man has been raised from the dead.

The discussion ends abruptly. The resurrection is absurd to the Athenians. Their philosophers have taught that the body is evil, a prison for the soul, and that death finally enables the soul to escape. The concept, then, that the body should be raised again and the soul live in it forever seems foolish.

It has by no means been Paul's most successful stop (17:32–34). Most sneer at his message. Others remain interested but unmoved; for them Paul's ideas are still just an academic curiosity (as in 17:21). Nevertheless, a few do come to faith, and the fact that two names are given suggests that they became prominent leaders in the church.

The other story in this week's session takes place five or six years later, after yet a third missionary journey by Paul (18:23–21:7). Returning to Jerusalem against the warning of his friends, Paul has been mobbed by angry Jews (21:27–30). They believe, incorrectly, that Paul has desecrated the temple by bringing Gentiles into it. This is the one offense for which the Romans would permit the Jews to execute a man, and they would have killed Paul had he not been taken into protective custody by the Roman commander (21:31–34; 23:10).

While Paul is being held in the Tower Antonia, a plot is devised to murder him (23:12–15). Sensing that they have no case against Paul, more than 40 men, likely of a group known as the Assassins, vow to kill him as he is being transferred for trial. (Such an oath would call down God's curse upon them should they fail.)

Somehow Paul's nephew (his sister's son) finds out about the plot (23:16–22). The commander takes the young man's tip very seriously (23:23–30). Immediately he resolves to send Paul to the Roman governor, Felix, in Caesarea. The commander is a chiliarch (an officer over 1,000 men), and he detaches nearly half his total force—200 foot soldiers, 70 cavalry, and 200 spearmen—to escort Paul out of Jerusalem. Because Paul is a Roman citizen, he is due the full rights and protection of the law (22:24–29). The commander, then, takes no chances of a lynching. He even bends the truth to take credit for his careful treatment of Paul (23:27).

Under cover of darkness, leaving about 9:00 p.m. (23:23), the troops conduct Paul safely to Antipatris and then to Caesarea, the Roman capital of Palestine (23:31–35). Here Paul would stay imprisoned for two years, facing trials before not only Felix, but also his successor Festus and King Herod Agrippa II (Acts 24–26).

Discussing the Text

1. Read Acts 17:16–26. What is significant about the place where Paul encounters the Athenians? What did they think of him? Why did they invite Paul to address them?

2. Read Acts 17:22–31. Paul abandons his usual methods and instead uses a style of argumentation familiar to the Athenians. Why would Paul do this?

3. Read Acts 17:32–34. What was the result of Paul's message to the Athenians?

4. Read 1 Corinthians 1:18–25. Contrast Paul's approach here with his approach in Acts 17.

5. Read Acts 21:26–33. Why was Paul imprisoned when he returned to Jerusalem?

6. Read Acts 23:16–22, 31–35. How is Paul rescued from the plot against his life?

7. Provide evidence of God at work in the life of Paul.

Apply

These stories of St. Paul, probably the greatest Christian missionary of all time, suggest important applications for us also hearing God's Word, sharing God's Word, and living God's Word. We learn from Paul's example in both Thessalonica and Athens how we can tailor the message and method to suit the particular audience. With Jews he began with the Old Testament; with Greeks he appealed to logic. This encourages us to consider how our friends are feeling—sad, angry, excited—when telling them about Jesus.

Yet Paul's experience in Athens also reminds us that only the actual word about Christ will ever win a soul. We can never reason, argue, or convince others to believe. And central to our sharing of Christ is the fact that Jesus is risen and living. We need not be discouraged if our witness is not believed; like Paul we will meet mixed results. But when we truly warn of sin and speak the comfort of Jesus' forgiveness, God will accomplish His results.

As hearers of the Word, we may be encouraged to follow the Bereans—to receive it eagerly and study it carefully. On the other hand, the Athenians illustrate the danger of placing our intelligence above God's Word, trusting only those things we can grasp with our own minds.

The Athenians also illustrate the emptiness of living without the hope God's Word brings. Those who do not know the true God ultimately live for nothing. Those who do know Him, though, may live every day without fear, for as God delivered Paul from the assassins in an unexpected way, so His Word assures us that He is always watching over us, even when we cannot see how.

1. Why is it important to tailor the message of Jesus Christ crucified to our audience? How might this be important for you? For your congregation?

2. How can the Athenians' response to Paul's message provide us comfort and hope when we witness about our faith in Jesus to unbelievers?

3. Describe the emptiness people have when they live without the hope that God's Word brings.

4. How might your congregation and congregational members more effectively share the Gospel with members of your community?

Catechism Connection

Examine the First Commandment and Luther's explanation in the opening for this session.

1. Read Philippians 2:1–11. According to verses 10–11, how do we show the importance of God in our lives?

2. How will this attitude affect other relationships (verses 3–4)?

3. With what power are we able to live this way (verse 1)?

Send

To Do This Week

Family Connection

1. Review with your family the events of the missionary journeys of Paul. Ask, "How does it feel when we share Jesus with a friend or loved one and he or she doesn't willingly receive it? How does Paul's experience with the Athenians give us comfort and hope?"

2. Consider what life would be like without Jesus. Then have each person complete the following sentence starter: "Because of Jesus, I ..." If time permits, have family members draw posters or pictures to illustrate their answers.

3. Pray together. Each person in the family should complete the following: "Thank You, Jesus, for ..."

For Personal Reflection

1. Consider the word *empty*. Meditate on how Jesus emptied Himself of His glory when He suffered and died on the cross and how by His emptying, you who were empty because of sin received the fullness of life.

2. Share with someone who does not know Jesus the reason for the hope that you have.

3. Pray that the Holy Spirit would empower you to witness boldly about your faith in Christ Jesus this week.

For Next Week

Read Acts 27:1–28:31 in preparation for next week's session.

Session 9

God Preserves Paul
from a Shipwreck

(Acts 27:1–28:31)

Gather

Theme: Who's in Control?

Key Point

God's unchanging and unending love for us gives us the assurance that He is with us always, even as we face disaster.

Objectives

By the power of the Holy Spirit working through God's Word, we will
1. summarize the miraculous events leading up to and including the shipwreck of Paul that demonstrated God's control;
2. describe how God used calamity to further spread the story of His love in Jesus; and
3. learn to face difficult situations in our lives with the confidence that God is in control and uses all situations for His good.

Opening

Read Martin Luther's explanation of the benefits of Baptism responsively.

Leader: What benefits does Baptism give?

Participants: It works forgiveness of sins, rescues from death and the devil, and gives eternal salvation to all who believe this, as the words and promises of God declare.

Leader: Which are these words and promises of God?

Participants: Christ our Lord says in the last chapter of Mark: "Whoever believes and is baptized will be saved, but whoever does not believe will be condemned." [Mark 16:16]

Introduction

A popular bumper sticker reads, "If you believe God is far away, guess who moved!"

1. Summarize the message of this bumper sticker.

2. If you feel comfortable doing so, share a time when the truth of this message became evident in your life.

The truth is that God doesn't move. We do. We distance ourselves from God as we miss opportunities to hear His Word or receive His body and His blood in the Lord's Supper. God is always in control. In today's session Paul faces hardships beyond measure, but through them all God demonstrates His control. God will accomplish His will and purpose. God uses even the most trying events to further spread His message of love and forgiveness through Jesus.

Study

Read aloud Acts 27:1–28:31.

Reading the Text

The entire book of Acts relates the drama of the Gospel spreading from Jerusalem to all Judea and Samaria and to the ends of the earth (Acts 1:8). In St. Paul's day, such an itinerary would naturally climax by reaching the "capital of the world," Rome. Apparently, for years Paul had hoped to preach there (Romans 1:11–15; 15:22–29). How, by God's grace, he safely arrived is quite a story!

One night during Paul's imprisonment in Jerusalem, Jesus appeared to him with the encouraging news that Paul would indeed testify about Him in Rome (Acts 23:11). After two years of detention under Felix, the opportunity finally came. The new governor, Festus, wished to return Paul from Caesarea to Jerusalem to stand trial before the Jews, but knowing the Jews' evil intent (25:3), Paul exercised his right as a Roman citizen: "I appeal to Caesar" (25:6–12). Though the governor knew Paul had committed no serious crime (26:30–32), he was therefore obligated to honor Paul's request. The apostle's trip to Rome would be financed by the state!

Of course, the voyage would be as a prisoner, but Paul was placed in the care of a centurion named Julius, who throughout the journey would show him kindness and respect (27:1–3, 31–32, 42–43). Paul was accompanied also by Luke, the author of Acts, and Aristarchus, who also would later be imprisoned with Paul (Acts 19:29; Acts 20:4; Colossians 4:10; Philemon 24).

Due to the prevailing winds, the west to east voyage across the Mediterranean was easy and direct, requiring not much more than two weeks. A trip in the opposite direction, however, was difficult and would take several times as long. It also required a round-about route, hugging the coast of Palestine and Syria northward, sailing around Cyprus, then heading westward past Asia Minor, which is present-day Turkey (Acts 27:4–8). During the first leg of the trip, Paul, Julius, and the others sailed aboard a ship from Adramyttium, a city in western Asia Minor. Next they transferred to a larger vessel, likely a grain ship from Alexandria in Egypt bound for Rome.

Unfortunately, the season was late; shipping virtually ceased from November to March because of deadly storms. It was already past the Day of Atonement ("the Fast," 27:9), late September or early October. It seemed wise to Paul, then, to spend the winter at the port they had now reached, Fair Havens, on the south of the island of Crete. Instead, the majority decided to risk reaching Phoenix, a better harbor on the same island (27:9–12).

The trip should have been only about 60 miles; it became 600. An initially favorable breeze changed suddenly to a wind of hurricane force sweeping down the mountains and into the sea (27:13–19). Luke's account of what follows is among the most detailed and realistic descriptions of a storm and shipwreck in ancient literature. The reader sees the crew strike the mainsail, secure the lifeboat, and pass cables under the hull to keep it from breaking up. They jettison most of the cargo as well as sails and spars, and they drop the sea anchor, which they hoped would catch and keep the ship from running aground should it approach dangerously shallow water. (Syrtis, 27:17, was a huge, infamous sandbar off North Africa. The crew feared they were that far off course!)

At this most desperate moment, God sends His reassurance. Not only will God's plan for Paul to reach Rome not fail, but all aboard will be spared for his sake. What a chance for Paul to witness about his faith to a receptive audience!

Only vaguely aware of their location after two weeks out of control, the crew finally senses they are near land, probably by the sound of breakers (27:27–29). Soundings confirm shallowing water, first 120 feet, then 90 feet.

But the crisis is not over. Soldiers and passengers could never have landed the ship without its crew, and the crew tries to escape. Again, the prisoner Paul, strengthened by the promise of God, encourages the mostly pagan travelers to keep the crew from leaving so that all will be saved. But now the final danger: making for the beach, the ship runs aground and will soon be smashed by the waves. There can be no organized way to bring everyone ashore; with every man for himself it seems certain that prisoners will scramble away and the soldiers will have to pay with their own lives. Yet, because he cares for Paul, Julius will not permit the prisoners to be executed. Instead, clearly by God's hand, all 276 persons swim or float to safety.

It turns out their landfall is the small island of Malta, just south of Sicily, near the "toe" of the Italian mainland. The islanders are kind, likely related to the great sailors, the Phoenicians, from the region of Tyre and Sidon. They immediately assist the castaways. Here Paul has another unexpected opportunity to witness (28:3–10). His own miraculous survival of the snakebite and his healings of others doubtless opened ears for his preaching of Christ.

As soon as the sailing season resumed, Paul's party was able to continue uneventfully on another Alexandrian ship (28:11–13). Ironically, it bore as its figurehead Castor and Pollux (Gemini, the Twins), the patron gods of sailors. Surely it had been no pagan god who had saved them from the sea!

Puteoli, on Naples Bay, was a major port for Rome, though several days south by land. "Brothers," fellow Christians, were already at Puteoli and at two other intermediate stops, eager to welcome Paul. Paul had reason to be encouraged. During his stay in Rome, in fact, Paul would have great freedom to visit with other believers and to preach.

One last time Paul began a mission stay by appealing to his fellow Jews (28:17–29). As usual, some believed, but many did not. Paul leaves them with a warning from their own Scriptures (Isaiah 6:9–10) that if they refuse to believe when God's message is preached, the opportunity will pass them by. Yet the book of Acts closes with the same great optimism with which it began: the Gospel will continue to go out to all nations, just as Jesus Himself had promised (Acts 28:28–31; 1:8).

While the Bible gives no further report of Paul's life, some of his letters imply (and tradition seems to confirm) that Paul was released after this two-year house arrest in Rome. Quite possibly he made further missionary journeys—to Spain (Romans 15:22–28) and again to Asia Minor. Following these, he was probably beheaded in Rome about the year A.D. 67 or 68 during the persecutions of Nero.

Discussing the Text

1. Read Acts 25:6–12; 26:32–27:1; and 28:14–16, 23–24. How did God enable Paul to finally preach in Rome?

2. Describe the events of the shipwreck (27:13–44).

3. How did God demonstrate His power in the events that occurred during the shipwreck?

4. The centurion refused to follow Paul's advice in Acts 27:9–12. How did God bring good out of this bad decision?

5. What "silent" demonstration of God's power do we find in Acts 27:33–36?

6. In what way can we consider Acts 28:23–24 to be a microcosm of Christian preaching?

7. How does the book of Acts close?

Apply

Two applications are most apparent in this week's story. First, Paul's voyage and shipwreck is a vivid illustration of God's uninterrupted protection. Not only is God always guarding His people from physical danger, but, much more important, He is constantly warding off Satan's spiritual threats. The Bible even speaks of the security Christ gives us in nautical terms, describing our hope in Christ as "an anchor of the soul" (Hebrews 6:17–20). We can always be certain that God is watching over us in even the most frightening circumstances.

Second, God makes clear that His Word will go out with its saving power wherever He intends. God arranged Paul's trip to Rome. God presented Paul with opportunities to witness aboard ship. And God made possible a most unlikely preaching station on Malta. Especially precious is the thought that Paul's escort, Julius, may have come to faith through his extended exposure to the apostle. How exciting it will be if we meet him in heaven! Likewise, God is continually opening doors for us to tell people about Christ. We can always speak with eagerness and confidence, knowing that God has created each new moment and will bless it according to His loving will.

1. How does God's action in the account of the shipwreck give us hope as we face physical danger? spiritual threats?

2. What does God's action in the account of the shipwreck tell about His ability to use hardships for His good? How does this give you comfort as you face hardships? See also Genesis 50:20 and Romans 8:28.

3. What doors has God opened to you in order for you to share the Good News of Jesus with others? How have you responded to these open doors?

4. "Any situation you encounter may be a door that God is opening for you to share the love of Jesus with others." If you affirm this statement, how will you approach new situations—both good and bad ones?

5. What encouragement related to sharing your faith do you find in Isaiah 55:11 and Hebrews 4:12?

Catechism Connection

Examine Luther's explanation of the benefits of Baptism responsively in the opening for this session.

1. God saves us through the water of Baptism (Mark 16:16; 1 Peter 3:20–21). How were people saved through the shipwreck of Acts 27?

2. In his Large Catechism (Part 239) Luther says that repentance is an effect of Baptism. How does Romans 2:4 support Luther's statement?

3. Why, then, was it proper for Peter to proclaim, "Repent and be baptized" (Acts 2:38)?

Send

To Do This Week

Family Connection

1. Read aloud dramatically the account of the shipwreck for your family. Then ask, "How did God use a dreadful situation to bring about good for many?"

2. Draw a picture depicting the shipwreck. Write the following caption on the picture: "An anchor of the soul!"

3. Share times when God has used difficult or troubling situations for your good and the good of your family.

For Personal Reflection

1. In a concordance, look for biblical references to nautical terms, for example, ship, anchor, boat, seas. How does God use these references to demonstrate power?

2. Consider the application of the account of the shipwreck to your life: (1) God guards His people from physical and spiritual danger; (2) God is in control and can use even the most difficult situations to His glory. Meditate on the importance of these scriptural truths for your life.

3. Share with a friend or loved one how God has used difficult times in your life to strengthen your faith.

For Next Week

Read Acts 1:1–14 in preparation for next week's session.

Session 10

Jesus Ascends into Heaven

(Acts 1:1–14)

Gather

Theme: God's Itinerary

Key Point

Jesus, who won the victory over sin, death, and the devil, is now seated at the right hand of God, where He exercises all authority over all creation. Therefore we can be confident that He is with us everywhere and at every moment.

Objectives

By the power of the Holy Spirit working through God's Word, we will
1. summarize the events of the ascension and Jesus' final instructions to His disciples;
2. describe how through the events of the ascension Jesus provides assurance of His presence—everywhere, at every moment; and
3. express with confidence the fact that Jesus is in control and with us always.

Opening

Pray together the Collect for the Ascension of Our Lord:

Grant, we pray, almighty God, that even as we believe Your only-begotten Son, our Lord Jesus Christ, to have ascended into heaven, so we may also in heart and mind ascend and continually dwell there with Him; who lives and reigns with You and the Holy Spirit, one God, now and forever. Amen.

Introduction

Jesus physically left His disciples when He ascended into heaven. One can only imagine that the disciples desired to keep Jesus with them. But God's itinerary would enable the blessings of forgiveness of sins and eternal life that Jesus won on the cross to extend beyond that which any human could imagine. In today's session we will explore God's purpose for Jesus' ascension as we witness the events surrounding the ascension.

1. How has your itinerary at times been different than God's itinerary for your life?

2. What might have occurred if you had followed your itinerary rather than God's?

3. How has God used His itinerary to bless your life?

Study

Read aloud Acts 1:1–14.

Reading the Text

In their worship services during these Sundays of the Easter season, many congregations have read Scripture lessons that have followed the spread of the resurrection message through the book of Acts. This week, the seventh and last Sunday of Easter, will be celebrated by many congregations as Ascension Sunday, remembering Christ's return to heaven in the first chapter of Acts. Our lesson, therefore, also takes us back to Christ's ascension, predating recent stories about Peter, Stephen, and Paul.

While it appropriately concludes the Easter season, Jesus' ascension is in a larger sense not an ending at all. Luke, the author of Acts, opens the book by saying that his first writing (the gospel of Luke) told only of what Jesus *began* to do and teach (Acts 1:1–2). Though Jesus will no longer be visibly present on earth, He will continue His work through His Word and Sacraments and those who bear them.

For 40 days since His resurrection, Jesus has been appearing to His disciples (Acts 1:3), leaving no doubt that He is really alive. (It is this 40-day period that our Easter season celebrates.) Several times, as promised, Jesus has appeared in Galilee (Matthew 28:7–10, 16–20; John 21:1–23). Now He gathers His followers in Jerusalem (Acts 1:4–5). The "Great Commissioning" in Matthew 28:16–20 should not be confused with the ascension, for the commissioning took place at one of these Galilean meetings days earlier. Jesus is preparing His disciples for Pentecost, the day when they will receive the Holy Spirit in Jerusalem. In the meantime, though, it is also from here that He will depart. He leads them out just to the east of the city, toward the ridge of the Mount of Olives (Acts 1:12) near Bethany (Luke 24:50).

Here Jesus has one last moment of instruction with His disciples. Since His resurrection, He has been explaining the true purpose of His coming—the forgiveness of sins (Luke 24:45–47). Even at this late date, however, the disciples remain fixated on His establishing an earthly kingdom (Acts 1:6). Jesus is gentle in His correction (1:7), not answering their question directly, but instead pointing to a higher goal: taking His salvation to the world. The itinerary He maps out will also become the outline of the book of Acts: first close to home base (Jerusalem), then in the surrounding regions (the rest of Judea and Samaria), and finally to the ends of the earth (1:8).

After He gives these instructions, Jesus raises His hands in blessing (Luke 24:50–51). As He does so, He is visibly lifted up into the sky until a cloud hides Him from the disciples' eyes (Acts 1:9). Jesus, of course, did not need to be physically elevated in order to enter heaven. In fact, in His state of exaltation (which began with His resurrection), Jesus constantly uses all of His divine attributes. The ascension enabled Jesus' disciples to grasp that His human nature was now also glorified. For that reason, it was also a fulfillment of Jesus' prayer in John 17:1–11.

With His ascension, Jesus took his seat "at the right hand" of God the Father (Ephesians 1:20–23). That is, Jesus, both in His divine and human natures, now exercises all authority over creation, at the behest of the Father. The right hand of God is not to be misunderstood as a place, as if Jesus' human body were now distant in heaven. (Some Christians incorrectly teach that Jesus' divine nature is everywhere but that His body is in heaven only.) Quite the contrary, the one Christ—both fully human and fully divine—is now omnipresent, rather than in one location only, as Jesus chose to be during His humiliation on earth.

Thus, as the disciples stared up into heaven they need not have felt like they were losing Jesus. He would truly be with them always. As the two "men" in white (angels) reminded them, He would one day return just as really, physically, and visibly as He had ascended.

The ascension story concludes with the little band living in joyful anticipation, praying and worshiping daily in the temple (Acts 1:12–14; Luke 24:52–53). The list of apostles and others (women, including Jesus' mother Mary, and His brothers, surely at least James and Jude) helps the reader likewise anticipate the day when this handful of faithful would be energized to change the world.

Discussing the Text

1. Why did Jesus command His followers, "Do not leave Jerusalem" (Acts 1:4)?

2. Had Jesus not given this command, what might the disciples have done?

3. Review Luke 24:27 and John 20:21–23. How does Acts 1:6 show that the disciples still didn't fully understand Jesus' mission?

4. How did Jesus respond to their question (Acts 1:7–8)?

5. How did Jesus in His response to the disciples map out the itinerary found in the book of Acts?

6. What assurance did the two "men" dressed in white give to the disciples (Acts 1:10–11)?

7. What evidences of Jesus' love for the disciples do you find in this account?

8. Compare Acts 1:9–11 with Hebrews 2:9. Describe the status of Jesus and the angels.

Apply

Jesus' ascension and seating at the right hand of God offer comforting applications for us. Perhaps most obviously, Jesus enters heaven as our forerunner. The fact that the human Christ was received into the glory of heaven vividly assures us that all who believe in Him will also ascend. Meanwhile, Jesus is preparing a place for each of us (John 14:2–3).

Second, since His ascension, Jesus has been and will continue to be with each of His children everywhere, at every moment. We may sometimes wish Jesus were with us visibly, but in fact it is so much better that He no longer limits Himself to a particular location. He is always present—both in His divinity and in His humanity. In a unique way, of course, this is especially true in Holy Communion as we receive the true body and blood of Christ. What a comfort to know Jesus is always with us!

Further, at the right hand of God, Jesus is constantly praying for us and for all believers (Romans 8:34). If we appreciate having others pray for us, how much more do we appreciate God's Son Himself interceding for us.

Finally, the ascended Christ, at God's right hand, rules all things on earth, including our lives, for the good of His church. Whatever happens, we can be certain of God's gracious results because Jesus is in charge (1 Peter 5:9–11). Thus, as we continue the work that Jesus began on earth, we can do so with confidence!

1. How does Jesus' ascension and seating at the right hand of God assure us of our future? See John 14:1–2.

2. Why is it better that Jesus ascended rather than stay with us on earth? See Matthew 18:20; 28:20; and Acts 18:10.

3. How is the Lord's Supper an assurance of Jesus' presence? See Matthew 26:26–28.

4. Why does Jesus in charge (sitting at the right hand of God) give us comfort and assurance no matter what situations we may encounter in this life? See Romans 8:34 and 1 Peter 5:9–11.

5. When do you feel especially grateful that Jesus ascended into heaven?

Catechism Connection

Examine the Second Article and Luther's explanation in the opening for Session 1.

1. In the Second Article we proclaim, "[Jesus] ascended into heaven and sits at the right hand of God, the Father Almighty." What insights into Jesus' role do you find in Ephesians 1:20–23?

2. Read Ephesians 4:10–12. How does Jesus sustain and build up His church?

3. Why are God's people able to carry out His work? (See, for example, John 16:7.)

Send

To Do This Week

Family Connection

1. Have your children draw a picture of Jesus' ascension. Label the picture with the words, "I am with you always."

2. Review the events surrounding the ascension. Discuss how these events continue to give us comfort as we live our lives on earth.

3. Create greeting cards to send to friends and family with the words "God is in control."

4. Discuss how Jesus is present with us today in His Word and in the Lord's Supper.

For Personal Reflection

1. Write the words "I am with you always" on a business card. Place the card in your wallet. When confronted with a difficult situation, you can pull out the card and read it.

2. Pray that God would continue to strengthen your faith as you study His Word.

3. Meditate on the magnitude of God's love for you—He does not leave you alone, but instead is with you always.

For Next Week

Read Acts 2:1–41; Joel 2:28–29; and John 16:5–11 in preparation for next week's session.

Session 11

The Holy Spirit Comes

(Acts 2:1–41; Joel 2:28–29; John 16:5–11)

Gather

Theme: Transformation

Key Point

God calls people to faith through the Gospel and, by the power of the Holy Spirit, transforms us from enemies of God to heirs who receive heaven.

Objectives

By the power of the Holy Spirit working through God's Word, we will

1. summarize the events of Pentecost and their significance;
2. list the four assertions Peter makes in his sermon;
3. affirm the power of the Holy Spirit working through the Gospel to transform us from enemies of God to heirs of heaven; and
4. proclaim boldly God's message of love and forgiveness through Jesus Christ.

Opening

Read the Third Article of the Apostles' Creed and Martin Luther's explanation responsively.

All: I believe in the Holy Spirit, the holy Christian church, the communion of saints, the forgiveness of sins, the resurrection of the body, and the life everlasting. Amen.

Leader: What does this mean?

Group 1: I believe that I cannot by my own reason or strength believe in Jesus Christ, my Lord, or come to Him; but the Holy Spirit has called me by the Gospel, enlightened me with His gifts, sanctified and kept me in the true faith.

Group 2: In the same way He calls, gathers, enlightens, and sanctifies the whole Christian church on earth, and keeps it with Jesus Christ in the one true faith.

Group 1: In this Christian church He daily and richly forgives all my sins and the sins of all believers.

Group 2: On the Last Day He will raise me and all the dead, and give eternal life to me and all believers in Christ.

All: This is most certainly true.

Introduction

Reflect upon the transforming work of the Holy Spirit in your life

• to transform you from a sinner doomed to eternal death to a saint who has received the gift of eternal life,

• to use you to share Jesus' love with others,

• to enable you to trust in God's plan for your life,

• to help you continue to grow in faith.

The power of the Holy Spirit was poured out upon the believers on Pentecost. God continues to unleash the transforming power of the Holy Spirit today through His Word and Sacraments in order to bring people to faith, to equip people for service, and to strengthen people's faith as they face the challenges of everyday life.

Study

Read Acts 2:1–41 and John 16:5–11.

Reading the Text

The little band of believers, just 120 of them at the time of Christ's ascension (Acts 1:15), would not be kept waiting long for the fulfillment of Jesus' parting promise. Ten days later on Pentecost, they are filled with the Holy Spirit and energized to carry Christ's message to the world.

During the brief interim, the disciples had been gathering in an upper room in Jerusalem, probably the same room in which Jesus had instituted His Supper (Acts 1:13; Mark 14:12–15). Besides prayer and daily worship in the temple, their one order of business had been to select Matthias as the replacement for Judas (Acts 1:15–26). Then came the day of Pentecost (Acts 2:1).

Pentecost was one of the three great festivals that God had established for Israel during their travels to the Promised Land (Leviticus 23:15–21). Also known as the Feast of Weeks or the Feast of Harvest, it was a kind of firstfruits thanksgiving at the time of the early wheat harvest, 50 days after Passover. (*Pentecost* comes from the Greek and means "fiftieth.") Therefore, it attracted to Jerusalem thousands of Jewish visitors "from every nation under heaven" (Acts 2:5), many of whom would have stayed the entire period since Passover.

Suddenly, early on this Pentecost, a sound like a "violent wind" swept through the city to the place the believers were assembled. As they looked about, they saw above their heads what appeared to be flames in the shape of tongues—appropriate shapes because of the miracle about to take place. Immediately, the disciples knew that this was the promised gift of the Holy Spirit. In Hebrew, the word for *wind* or *breath* is the same word as that for *spirit*; in the Old Testament it is sometimes used with this double meaning (e.g., Ezekiel 37:1–14). Fire was associated with the Holy Spirit (Matthew 3:11).

Certainly these disciples already possessed the Holy Spirit; every believer's faith is worked by the Spirit, who then dwells in the heart. In fact, the apostles themselves had received Him directly from Jesus (John 20:22–23). But now the Spirit would give special, new gifts appropriate to the situation. For this occasion, the most apparent gift was the ability of the believers to speak in foreign languages they had never learned (Acts 2:4).

The languages were the native dialects of all those visitors to Jerusalem (2:5–11), and are not to be confused with the speaking in unrecognizable tongues in Corinth (1 Corinthians 12–14). On this day, the audience clearly recognized and understood the words being spoken. The Holy Spirit had given the gift in order that the disciples could proclaim Christ. (It seems most likely that all 120 received this gift. However, when the moment for formal, public preaching arose, it was the apostles who spoke; Acts 2:14.)

Quickly a crowd gathered (2:12–13). Those who mocked were probably standing around the periphery and mistook the many languages for drunken babbling. The charge was easily dismissed; at this hour of the morning—the "third hour" or 9:00 A.M.—even those who might be given to wine would more likely be sleeping off the previous night's excesses.

Peter seizes the moment. These amazing phenomena, he says, are the fulfillment of Joel 2:28–32, for God was now pouring out His Spirit on all people. Beyond simply justifying the unusual events, though, Peter is introducing a powerful call to repentance. These are the last days, with the terrifying wonders of the end now imminent. It is high time to be prepared! And Peter is about to explain how they may call upon the Lord for salvation.

Peter's sermon develops around four assertions: (1) that by many miracles God testified to Jesus of Nazareth (Acts 2:22); (2) that Jesus' suffering was according to God's eternal plan (2:23a); (3) that "you" crucified Him (2:23b), and (4) that God raised and exalted Him (2:24). The first and third assertions required no proof, for they were common knowledge even among Jesus' enemies. Peter, therefore, proceeds to prove the second and fourth.

His evidence again comes from the Old Testament, which his hearers were bound to accept. He quotes Psalm 16:8–11, where David had declared that God would not abandon His Holy One to decay in the grave (Acts 2:25–28). Obviously, David was not speaking of himself, for everyone in Jerusalem could see that David was still dead and buried there (Acts 2:29). David must have been writing prophetically about his promised descendant, the Christ (Acts 2:30–31; Psalm 132:11). Clearly, then, God had planned—and revealed to David—the resurrection of the Messiah. This meant, of course, that Jesus' death was also according to God's plan. And if the people would simply remember the many attesting miracles of Jesus, they would understand that He must have been the promised Christ. Peter's assertions must be true! Jesus of Nazareth is risen and exalted to the right hand of God (Acts 2:32–33). His enemies are sure to be crushed under His feet (Acts 2:34–35; Psalm 110:1). He is Lord and Christ—"this Jesus, whom you crucified" (Acts 2:36).

The response is desperation. In effect, they ask, "Are we done for, then?" Could there be any hope for those who have committed the worst sin possible? Absolutely. In fact, Peter assures, in repentance and Baptism there is forgiveness of all sins for everyone, everywhere (Acts 2:38–39). Not only is this a powerful statement that Baptism forgives sins, but it also demonstrates that infants are to receive the blessing of Baptism. Peter and the disciples had once been rebuked by Jesus for keeping little children away (Mark 10:13–16). Now the invitation—on God's authority—is "for you and your children," an invitation for persons of all ages.

The preaching of the Word, empowered by the Spirit, resulted in 3,000 converts (Acts 2:40–41). And this was only the beginning. Aptly, Pentecost is celebrated as the "birthday of the church."

Discussing the Text

1. How does Leviticus 23:15–21 explain the gathering in Acts 2:1, 5?

2. Describe the significance of the Holy Spirit coming in wind and fire (Acts 2:2–4).

3. What gift from the Holy Spirit was most apparent on the day of Pentecost (Acts 2:6–7)? How is this gift different from "speaking in tongues"?

4. Read Joel 2:28–32. Why was it appropriate for Peter to quote this verse to the people (Acts 2:17–21)?

5. What were Peter's assertions in the following portions of his sermon: Acts 2:22; 2:23a; 2:23b; 2:24–36?

6. What is the good news in 2:37?

7. What further evidence of the Holy Spirit's power do we find in 2:41?

Apply

The miracle of Pentecost shows in a dramatic way the transforming power of the Holy Spirit. By the Spirit's power, cowering disciples became fearless witnesses, and avowed enemies of Christ became believers in the Gospel. This can be a tremendous encouragement to us. Those who feel too shy to speak of Christ may be assured that the Holy Spirit will speak through them. Another wonderful name for the Holy Spirit is variously translated "Counselor," "Comforter," "Helper," "Intercessor," or "Advocate" (John 16:7). It literally means "one called to stand alongside." The Holy Spirit is always standing beside us as we tell of Jesus.

We may be further assured that the Spirit is working to melt the resistance of those to whom we speak. The Spirit can convict the hearts of even the most hardened unbelievers (John 16:8–11). We need never give up witnessing to friends, family, or acquaintances no matter how disinterested they may seem.

Another important application of the Pentecost story is the certainty of forgiveness it offers. As we repent, our Baptism forgives even our worst sins. If murdering Jesus was forgiven in Baptism, our sins surely are also.

Finally, we are strengthened by a sense of fellowship with the ancient church. As Christians, we are members of a great and historic body, born in dramatic fashion by the Holy Spirit's miraculous power. Should we ever feel ashamed of the church in a world that often denigrates it, we may take heart in remembering its powerful origin.

1. Describe the transforming power of the Holy Spirit unleashed on the day of Pentecost. Describe the transforming power of the Holy Spirit unleashed at your Baptism. See Romans 6:3–8.

2. How does the Holy Spirit empower us to share the love of Christ? How does the Holy Spirit work on the hearts of those with whom we share God's love?

3. What certainty does Pentecost provide you concerning the forgiveness of your sins? See Colossians 2:11–12 and 1:13–14.

4. How are we strengthened as we consider the line of faithful Christians who have gone before us?

5. From generation to generation the Holy Spirit has led Christians to share the love of Christ. Describe how that power has been evident as others have shared that message with you or as you have shared it with others.

Catechism Connection

Examine the Third Article and Luther's explanation in the opening for this session.

1. The Article begins, "I believe in the Holy Spirit, the holy Christian church, the communion of saints." What is the connection between the Holy Spirit and the Christian church, or the communion of saints?

2. Read Romans 8:4–9. What change does the Holy Spirit work in you?

3. Read Romans 8:26–27. What comfort and assurance do these words give?

Send

To Do This Week

Family Connection

1. Create a family picture of the events that occurred on Pentecost. Label the picture "Transforming Power."

2. Pull out memorabilia to help members of your family remember the day of their Baptism. Remind family members that on the day of their Baptism, the Holy Spirit transformed them from enemies of God to heirs of heaven.

3. Have a Baptism birthday party for the members of your family.

4. Discuss how the Holy Spirit continues to empower us today to share Jesus' love and forgiveness with others. Share the names of people who need to hear of the love of Jesus.

For Personal Reflection

1. Review Peter's sermon. Consider each of the assertions he made in his sermon.

2. Meditate on the love of God that transformed you at your Baptism.

3. Share confidently the love of God in Christ Jesus with someone who has not experienced the transforming power of the Holy Spirit. Be assured that God's work will accomplish its purpose, even if the person doesn't respond as you might desire.

For Next Week

Read Matthew 25:31–46 and 28:16–20 in preparation for the next session.

Session 12

Jesus Will Take Us to Heaven

(Matthew 25:31–46; 28:16–20)

Gather

Theme: Celebrate!

Key Point

For those who possess saving faith in Jesus Christ, God provides complete assurance that on Judgment Day we will enjoy the blessings of eternal life in heaven because Jesus completely paid the price for our sin through his death on the cross.

Objectives

By the power of the Holy Spirit working through God's Word, we will

1. summarize Jesus' message to believers and unbelievers concerning Judgment Day;
2. describe how Jesus Himself fulfills the work He describes in the Great Commission;
3. celebrate the certainty of eternal life won by Jesus on the cross; and
4. share boldly the reason for our joy-filled anticipation of Judgment Day.

Opening

Read together the Apostles' Creed.

I believe in God, the Father Almighty, Maker of heaven and earth.

And in Jesus Christ, His only Son, our Lord, who was conceived by the Holy Spirit, born of the Virgin Mary, suffered under Pontius Pilate, was crucified, died and was buried. He descended into hell. The third day He rose again from the dead. He ascended into heaven and sits at the right hand of

God, the Father Almighty. From thence He will come to judge the living and the dead.

I believe in the Holy Spirit, the holy Christian church, the communion of saints, the forgiveness of sins, the resurrection of the body, and the life everlasting. Amen.

Introduction

1. What events have you celebrated recently?

2. What are the reasons for celebrating these events?

3. How might people respond if you had a celebration for the coming of Judgment Day? Why would they respond in this way?

In today's session we study Jesus' words to us about Judgment Day. Judgment Day for us who possess saving faith in Jesus provides reason to celebrate. We will also see how through our celebration of the upcoming Judgment Day we can witness boldly about the reason for our confidence, peace, and joy to those who anticipate that day in terror. Our faith in Jesus gives us this peace.

Study

Read aloud Matthew 25:31–46 and 28:16–20.

Reading the Text

Since Advent, the church calendar has, for the most part, followed the great events in the life of Jesus. Now that we have seen Christ ascend back to heaven and send His Holy Spirit to ignite the church in its mission, we come to Trinity Sunday, a celebration of the work and essence of the Father, Son, and Holy Spirit.

Jesus' most detailed description of Judgment Day (Matthew 25:31–46) climaxes a lengthy discourse on the end times that He delivered just days before He died. At a moment when He is least expected (24:36–44), Jesus will physically and visibly descend from the clouds of heaven and take His seat on the throne of judgment (Matthew 25:31; Revelation 20:11–12). Angels will trumpet His return (Matthew 24:30–31). All people, both those living at the time and those who have died (1 Thessalonians 4:16–17), will be gathered before Him. (The bodies of those who have died will at this instant be raised and reunited with their souls; John 5:28–29.) Significantly, Jesus here calls Himself the Son of Man, because it links the passage to Old Testament prophecy (Daniel 7:9, 13–14) and emphasizes that, although He would soon be killed, Christ was already glorified in His human nature (Matthew 26:64–66).

Immediately, before any discussion takes place, Jesus will separate all people groups into two; no one will be able to remain neutral. The shepherd-sheep-goats illustration is useful not only because such culling was a real practice (see Ezekiel 34:17–22), but also because it recalls Jesus' tender role as the Good Shepherd who died to save the sheep (John 10:11). Judgment Day is not Jesus' first appearance to mankind; He has already done everything possible to prepare us for this day.

The separation of sheep from goats is determined by one criterion: faith in Jesus or lack thereof. His sheep have heard His voice, He knows them, and they have followed Him (John 10:14, 27–28). Those who did not believe in Him were never His sheep (John 10:25–26). What comes next, therefore, must not be misconstrued as in any way teaching salvation by good works.

It is instead evidence of faith or unbelief that the world can see. The King cites the works or absence of works of each group, beginning with the believers (Matthew 25:34–36). Jesus sees directly into hearts; He has been able to make the correct division already. But for human beings, who can see only the works that faith brings, examples are listed. Faith in Jesus will always motivate believers to do good works, however imperfect. Lack of faith makes it impossible to do anything truly good (Hebrews 11:6).

The good works of believers may not seem impressive. In fact, Christ's sheep will be unaware they were doing anything for Him (Matthew 25:37–39). But because these deeds were motivated by faith, and carried out for the benefit of Christ's people ("brothers of Mine"), they were done for Christ. How comforting to notice, too, that while believers also constantly sinned, failing to do good, those failures are never mentioned. The believers are blessed by the Father because their sins are forgiven by faith in Christ.

By stark contrast, the only evidence that can be cited in the case of unbelievers is their lack of any good works. Because they did not believe in Jesus, they never did anything for Christ. Even deeds of charity or outward kindness that would have seemed noteworthy have been worthless before God because they came from corrupt hearts. And, remarkably, it will be quite unnecessary to mention the sinful acts that unbelievers did commit, since everything they did was sin.

The separation of sheep and goats becomes eternal (Matthew 25:46). Unbelievers are condemned to everlasting fire—this is tragic, since hell had been intended only for the devil and his angels. But Christians enter into the joys of heaven, which God has been preparing for them from creation. "And so we will be with the Lord forever" (1 Thessalonians 4:17).

Meanwhile, Jesus continues to be with us, as He assured the disciples a few days before His ascension (Matthew 28:16–20). In giving the Great Commission, Jesus also gave pledge that the full power and presence of the Holy Trinity would go with us to make disciples of all nations.

As promised on Easter, Jesus met the Eleven (Judas was dead and Matthias had not yet been chosen) on a mountain in Galilee. Now in His state of exaltation, He was fully authorized to direct the remainder of human history. The Great Commission was the key.

The Great Commission would be fulfilled by two means, both in which Christ Himself works. First, baptizing makes disciples (Matthew 28:19). Baptism creates new disciples by bringing souls into the family of God, giving them His name. Baptizing "in the name of" the triune God also means that the apostles—or pastors or lay persons—would only be visible stand-ins for God; God Himself is actually doing the baptizing. Thus Baptism certainly gives all the blessings God promises—faith, forgiveness, and eternal life (Titus 3:5, Acts 2:38, 1 Peter 3:21). (Baptism is clearly intended especially for infants because they are included among "all nations.")

Second, the verbal proclamation of the Gospel, "teaching," makes and strengthens disciples (Matthew 28:20a). Every point of doctrine ("everything I have commanded") contributes to active discipleship. Again, the teaching of Christ's Word is in fact Christ Himself speaking.

Christ's closing blessing, then, follows quite naturally. Jesus would be with us always, not only as a matter of His omnipresence, but, more vitally, in His means of grace. He is, of course, every-where all the time. But He is with His church personally, and pow-erfully, in Baptism, Holy Communion, and the Word.

Discussing the Text

1. Read Matthew 24:36–44. What had Jesus emphasized about Judgment Day in these verses?

2. What details does Jesus add in Matthew 25:31–44?

3. Compare Matthew 25:32–33 with John 10:14, 25–29. What is the significance of Jesus' metaphor of sheep and goats? What is the difference between a sheep and a goat?

4. What is the difference between a good work done by a believer and a good work performed by an unbeliever?

5. How do Jesus' words in Matthew 25:34–40 support the fact that we are saved by faith, not by works?

6. How is the Great Commission (Matthew 28:19–20) fulfilled by Christ Himself?

7. How is Jesus with His church today?

Apply

Many applications may be drawn from these lessons. The certainty of final judgment makes the task of the Great Commission pressing. All of our friends and family members will stand before Christ and be placed either to His right or His left. Christ has called each of us to be His voice to these people we know.

At the same time, hearing Jesus describe Judgment Day can relieve anxieties we may have about the end of the world. Sensational, nonbiblical speculations of the end are all too common, particularly in certain religious media. We have God's own Word that Jesus will be with us to the very end and that there will be no surprises on the Last Day for those who trust in Him.

Of course, Jesus' listing of the kind deeds of believers calls us to acts of charity. We can, by the Spirit's power, care for the hungry and thirsty, the homeless and poor, the sick and the prisoner. While such actions do not earn God's favor, they are joyous fruits of faith. We receive special pleasure as we are reminded of Jesus' words, "You did [it] for Me."

Next, Christ's presence with us becomes more tangible when located in the Word and Sacraments. He is not "with you always" in some vague sense. He is speaking when the pastor speaks, touching when the water drips, on the tongue when the bread and wine are received. His guidance, forgiveness, and eternal life are also there in these means.

Finally, we who believe cannot think of Judgment Day without looking ahead to the glories of heaven. On that day we will all be changed (1 Corinthians 15:51–53), having our bodies transformed to be like Christ's resurrected body (Philippians 3:20–21). While heaven will surpass description, it will be rich and beautiful, without death or sadness of any kind (Revelation 21:10–22:5). We will rejoice in worship with all the saints. Best of all, we will be with Jesus Himself forever.

1. Why is Judgment Day and the uncertainty of the day of its coming important to us as we consider friends and family members who do not possess saving faith in Jesus?

2. How does Jesus' description of Judgment Day relieve the fears of those who believe in Him?

3. How can we respond to Jesus' love for us?

4. Why does Jesus' presence become tangible to us as we hear His Word and receive His body and blood in the Lord's Supper?

5. Read 2 Timothy 4:1–8, words that Paul wrote when he knew his life would soon end. What are some important things he wanted Timothy to know?

Catechism Connection

Examine the Apostles' Creed in the opening for this session.
1. Who are the three persons of the Trinity as revealed in the Creed?

2. With what work do we associate each member of the Trinity?

3. Why is it important that the Creed is faithful to Scripture? See 2 Timothy 3:15.

Send

To Do This Week

Family Connection

1. Ask each family member to describe heaven. Or have family members draw pictures of what they think heaven looks like.

2. Tell members of the family that Jesus is present in Word and Sacrament. Ask, "Why is it important that we constantly hear and study God's Word? Why is it important that we regularly receive the Lord's Supper?"

3. Pray daily for those family members or friends who do not know Jesus as Lord and Savior. Ask that the Lord would provide you opportunities to share His love with them.

For Personal Reflection

1. Reread Jesus' description of Judgment Day. Say a prayer thanking God for the gift of saving faith by which you are assured of eternal life.

2. Meditate on Jesus' presence with us today in Word and Sacrament. Seek new opportunities to experience God's presence through Word and Sacrament.

3. Consider the verbs in the Great Commission (e.g., go, make, baptizing, teaching). How can you fulfill that which Jesus commands us to do?

For Next Week

Read Luke 10:1–24 and Matthew 5:13–20 in preparation for next week's session.

Session 13

Jesus Sends Workers into His Harvest Field

(Luke 10:1–24; Matthew 5:13–20)

Gather

Theme: Equipped

Key Point

God commanded all He has called to faith in Christ Jesus to tell others of His great love for them.

Objectives

By the power of the Holy Spirit working through God's Word we will

1. describe the significance of Jesus sending out the 70;
2. confess our failure to tell others of Jesus' love;
3. rejoice in the forgiveness Jesus won for us on the cross, including our unwillingness to witness His love boldly;
4. tell others of God's love for us in Christ Jesus.

Opening

Read the Second Petition of the Lord's Prayer and Martin Luther's explanation responsively.

All: Thy kingdom come.

Leader: What does this mean?

Group: The kingdom of God certainly comes by itself without our prayer, but we pray in this petition that it may come to us also.

Leader: How does God's kingdom come?

Group: God's kingdom comes when our heavenly Father gives us His Holy Spirit, so that by His grace we believe His holy Word and lead godly lives here in time and there in eternity.

Introduction

"I'm equipped to (for) …"

1. How might you finish that sentence starter? List as many endings as possible.

2. How did you become equipped for each of the things you listed?

3. How would you respond to the following statement: "I am fully equipped to tell others of Jesus' love for me"?

In today's lesson we will recognize that God is the equipper. God has and will equip all who have received the gift of saving faith in Christ Jesus to tell others of the person and work of Jesus on their behalf.

Study

Read Luke 10:1–24 and Matthew 5:13–20.

Reading the Text

Since faith in Jesus is the only way of salvation, there is no greater task than spreading His Gospel. For that task, there is always a need for more workers.

Not long before today's story, Jesus had sent the Twelve out to preach, heal, and exorcize demons in the cities of Galilee (Luke 9:1–6; Matthew 9:37–10:23; Mark 6:7–13). Now, as He plans His final journey to Jerusalem (Luke 9:51), He sends 70 men (some versions read 72) to announce Him in the cities He will soon visit

(10:1)—cities of Perea (east of the Jordan) and Judea (to the south, surrounding Jerusalem).

The number 70 (or 72) is significant. While 12 had represented the heads of the 12 tribes of Israel, 70 was a symbolic number for the whole nation. Seventy was also the number of elders once appointed to assist Moses (Numbers 11:16). Alternatively, the Jews thought of 72 as the count of all non-Jewish nations of the world. The point, with either number, was that this field was much larger than could be harvested by the apostles alone (Luke 10:2). (For other illustrations of winning souls as reaping a harvest, see Matthew 13:24–30, 36–43 and John 4:35–38.)

The 70 were to go out in the simplest—almost naive—faith, as lambs among wolves, without even basic necessities (Luke 10:3–8). They were to trust that God would lead them to food and housing. They were not to move from house to house, seeking better accommodations, as did many later itinerant "apostles" (2 Corinthians 11:4–13).

Along with the power to heal, the 70 were given authority to proclaim the same message Jesus and John the Baptist before Him had preached: "The kingdom of God has come near to you!" (Luke 10:9; cf. Matthew 3:2; 4:17; Mark 1:15; Luke 4:43) It was a message of both Law and Gospel. To all who would receive Christ as the promised Savior, it would be God's word of peace (10:5–6), for Jesus would reconcile God and humanity by His death.

But to those who would reject Christ, the coming of the Kingdom would be a sign of judgment (10:10–16). Having had Christ so near would only increase their responsibility. Korazin and Bethsaida, both towns of Galilee, and Capernaum, Jesus' adopted home, had been the very centers of His activity. Their rejection of Christ, therefore, would bring punishment even greater than that of notorious Sodom (Genesis 19:1–29) or of the pagan cities of Tyre and Sidon, which had heard little of the Messiah.

Such will always be the effect of God's Word. Some will believe and be saved; others will reject and become all the more guilty. And this, Jesus says, will become visible in people's reactions to His ambassadors, because speaking His Word gives them the very same authority as Christ Himself (Luke 10:16). As comfort, this assures that the preaching of forgiveness is as certain as if Jesus

Himself pronounced it. As warning, it cautions that the voice of the church and its ministers is to be taken seriously when from Scripture it condemns sin.

We are not told how long the mission of the 70 lasted, but they return exuberant at the authority of that Word (10:17–19). Even the demons must obey when they speak in Christ's name, for Jesus has conquered the prince of demons, Satan. (Satan's "fall like lightning from heaven," 10:18, is a figurative description of his defeat by Jesus' perfect obedience, death, and resurrection.) Armed with Christ's Word, Jesus' disciples have the same power over the devil (Romans 8:37–39).

As exciting as was this power over evil spirits, Jesus reminds His disciples that it is not the greatest reason to rejoice. The greatest joy of a disciple is still always the most basic—a place in heaven (10:20; cf. Daniel 12:1; Hebrews 12:22–23; Revelation 20:12, 21:27).

The mission of the 70 is complete, and Jesus rejoices greatly (Luke 10:21–24). The message of salvation has gone out in all its simplicity and power. Those who are too proud or too full of their own wisdom to see their need for a Savior will miss it. But those who, like children, receive what they are given with humble trust will now have the privilege of knowing God. How blessed Jesus' disciples are to see these things happen—and to have a part in making them happen!

Discussing the Text

1. Read Matthew 5:14–16. What role in His mission does Jesus give to all His followers?

2. Read Luke 9:1–2 and 10:1–2. What steps did Jesus take to enlarge His church?

3. Jesus sends out 70 men to announce Him in the cities He will soon visit. What is significant of the number 70?

4. Read Luke 10:3–7. How were the 70 to go out? What is significant about the way Jesus commanded them to go out?

5. Read Luke 10:8–16. What power and authority were the men given by Jesus?

6. Read Luke 10:17–20. What were the effects of God's Word on people? How are these effects still evident today?

7. What is the greatest joy of a disciple of Jesus? Why?

Apply

The lesson of the 70 is that evangelism—spreading the Gospel—is the Lord's mandate to the church. It is not the "job" of professional, full-time church workers only. It is the calling and responsibility of every Christian. Just as Jesus—and even the Twelve—could not go everywhere, we have friends, family, and co-workers that no one else can reach.

As we go into our personal harvest fields, we can expect difficulties. We can expect rejection. But we can also expect success. And we can be certain that the Lord of the harvest will be with us, for we are on His errand. What a privilege!

1. Whose responsibility is it to share the Gospel? See Matthew 5:14–16 and Acts 1:8.

2. Who among your family and friends needs to hear of the love and forgiveness Jesus has won for them on the cross? In what ways might you share the Gospel with that person?

3. What can we expect as we share Jesus' love and forgiveness with others? What can we expect from Jesus as we share His message?

4. Write a prayer confessing that you often fail to witness to others. Thank Jesus for the forgiveness He earned for you on the cross for this sin and all others. Pray that the Holy Spirit would empower you to witness Jesus' love boldly. Plan to share your prayer during the week with your family and use it in your own personal devotional time.

Catechism Connection

Examine the Second Petition of the Lord's Prayer and Luther's explanation in the opening for this session.

1. Compare Luther's description of your role in God's kingdom with Jesus' words in Matthew 5:16. Why is that role important (Romans 10:14)?

2. How does God equip you for your role in His kingdom? See 2 Timothy 3:14–17.

3. Why need we not get discouraged, even when people reject us because we are sharing our faith? See 2 Timothy 4:18.

Send

To Do This Week

Family Connection
1. Review the story of the sending of the 70. Remind your family that all who possess faith in Jesus have been given the power to share His love with others.

2. Give each family member an opportunity to share what the forgiveness of sins and eternal life that Jesus won for her on the cross means to her.

3. Pray the prayer you wrote earlier.

4. Make a list of your non-Christian friends and acquaintances. Pray for each of these people. Pray also that God would provide you the opportunity and power to share your faith in Jesus with these people.

For Personal Reflection
1. Pray daily the prayer you wrote earlier.

2. Make a list of people with whom you come into contact who do not confess Jesus as their Savior. Select at least one with whom you will share your faith this week.

Adult Leader Guide

Session 1

Jesus Talks about Greatness

(Matthew 18:1–9; 20:17–28)

Gather

Theme: Who Is the Greatest?

Key Point and Objectives

Invite volunteers to read aloud the key point and objectives for this session.

Opening

Read aloud in unison the Second Article of the Apostles' Creed and Luther's explanation to the article.

Then lead the group in prayer: Thank You, dear Savior, for the salvation You have earned for us. May the power of the Spirit lead us to recognize that through faith in You we have already received true greatness, and may we respond to that gift with joyful service to You and others. We pray in Your name. Amen.

Introduction

Read emphatically the question. Then discuss the questions that follow. If your class is large, you may want to assign participants to small groups so that all have an opportunity to share.

1. Answers will vary. Make sure participants back up their responses with reasons. This will enable you to create a list of characteristics usually associated with greatness.

2. Answers will vary. Refer to the reasons that participants identified people as great.

Read aloud the closing paragraph of this section.

Study

Read aloud Matthew 18:1–9; 20:17–28 and the commentary.

Discussing the Text

1. Even though the disciples argued about greatness after Jesus talked about His death, they must have known it was wrong to do so, for they kept quiet when Jesus asked what they were arguing about.

2. Children are dependent on others for all things. Therefore, a person who is great in God's eyes is the one who depends upon God for all things. The truly great person relies fully on God's greatness for physical and spiritual life.

3. Jesus emptied Himself of all of His glory and then went willingly to the cross to suffer and to die for the sins of all people.

4. James and John obviously believe that Jesus' kingdom will be like an earthly kingdom where the Messiah would be a great earthly conqueror and usher in the age of freedom and perfection, and where certain people would hold more exalted positions. The disciples do not understand that greatness in the kingdom of God means willingly giving up everything, including their lives.

5. Answers may vary. True greatness is marked by service that seeks nothing for itself. Jesus demonstrates true greatness—the only thing He received for His perfect life was death on the cross. He died for others.

Apply

Read aloud the opening paragraphs. Then discuss the questions that follow.

1. Answers will vary. Any thoughts, words, and actions that put ourselves above others are self-centered.

2. Jesus empowers us for service by His love demonstrated for us on the cross. We serve God and others in spontaneous gratitude for all that Jesus has done for us.

3. When we confess our sinful self-centeredness, we admit to God that we have fallen short of His expectations for our lives— we have put ourselves first, and others and Him second. Remind participants that if we put ourselves first, then others come last. Jesus provides complete forgiveness to all who confess their sins

to Him. We respond to the love and forgiveness Jesus provides to us by loving, forgiving, and serving others.

4. God made us "alive with Christ" (Ephesians 2:5). His grace moves us to *want* to "do good works" (2:10)—to be involved in service to God and others.

Catechism Connection

1. Paul's words in Ephesians 2:1–3 describe our condition under the power of the devil. Verses 4–10 describe our "redeemed" condition.

2. Christ has freed us from the slavery of sin, and He has rescued us from death and from the power of the devil.

Send

Urge participants to complete one or more of the "Family Connection" activities and one or more of the "For Personal Reflection" activities prior to the next time you meet. Then close with prayer.

For Next Week

Urge participants to read Matthew 21:1–11; 27:45–66 in preparation for the next session.

Session 2

Jesus Enters Jerusalem

(Matthew 21:1–11; 27:45–66)

— Gather —

Theme: His Primary Purpose

Key Point and Objectives

Invite a different volunteer to read aloud the key point and each of the objectives.

Opening

Read the Second Commandment and Luther's explanation responsively. Then lead the group in prayer: Dear God, preserve us from the temptations to misuse Your name. Lead us instead to proclaim to a world dead in sin that "I resolved to know nothing ... except Jesus Christ and Him crucified" (1 Corinthians 2:2). In His name we pray. Amen.

Introduction

Discuss the questions. If your class is large, you may want to assign participants to small groups so that all have a chance to share.

1. Answers will vary. A waiter serves food. A comedian entertains. A physician diagnoses and heals. A parent nurtures and guides his or her children. A teacher teaches.

2. Again, answers may vary. After participants have shared their responses, tell them that the primary reason Jesus came to earth was to fulfill the Law perfectly in our place and to suffer, die, and rise again for the sins of all people.

3. The primary purpose of the Christian church is to proclaim Jesus Christ crucified to a world lost in sin.

Read aloud the closing paragraph of this section.

Study

Read aloud or invite volunteers to read aloud portions of Matthew 21:1–11; 27:45–66 and the commentary.

Discussing the Text

1. Jesus ultimately came to earth for only one purpose—to die on the cross.

2. The triumphal entry into Jerusalem was a step toward suffering. Jesus' enemies became more furious by the commotion He created. They determined to find a way to discredit Jesus and, ultimately, do away with the problem.

3. "Hosanna" is a prayer that means "Save now!" Perhaps many in the crowd were more interested in salvation from the Romans than in salvation from sin, death, and the devil.

4. Jesus' enemies were furious with Jesus' entry into Jerusalem.

5. People thought that Jesus would establish an earthly kingdom that would overthrow the Roman occupation and restore the people of Israel to the glory that they had once known.

Apply

Invite a different volunteer to read aloud each of the paragraphs in this section. Then discuss the questions that follow.

1. Although Jesus was a great prophet, taught us about living, and provided an example of moral living, all of these focuses lose sight of the real purpose of Jesus' coming to earth. The primary purpose Jesus came to earth was to die and rise again for our sins. Any emphasis other than His bloody death on the cross to win for us forgiveness of sins can cause us to lose sight of the primary message of the Christian church—Jesus Christ crucified.

2. On the cross Jesus became an acceptable sacrifice for our sins. The cross is the primary focus of the Christian church, because through the Gospel—Jesus Christ crucified—the Holy Spirit works to create and to strengthen saving faith through which we receive the blessing of eternal life.

3. Jesus' miracles, teaching, and life are all seen through the cross. Everything Jesus did and said was ultimately to point us to the sacrifice He would endure for us on the cross.

4. "Jesus Christ crucified" is the essence of the Christian church. The church's primary mission is to proclaim the forgiveness of sins and eternal life that Jesus won for all people when He suffered and died on the cross and rose from the dead.

5. Answers will vary. Provide ample opportunity for participants to share with each other the meaning of the cross in their lives.

Catechism Connection

1. God forbids calling on spiritists, horoscopes, and similar ways to foretell the future.

2. Answers will vary.

3. God invites us to turn to Him in prayer. He holds the future in His hands.

Send

Urge participants to complete one or more of the "Family Connection" activities and one or more of the suggested "For Personal Reflection" activities during the week. Then close with prayer.

For Next Week

Urge participants to read Matthew 26:57–66 in preparation for next week's session.

Session 3

Church Leaders Condemn Jesus

(Matthew 26:57–66)

Gather

Theme: The Tables Are Turned!

Key Point and Objectives

Invite volunteers to read aloud the key point and each of the objectives.

Opening

Read the Eighth Commandment and Luther's explanation responsively. Then lead the group in prayer: Dear Jesus, Your love for us motivates us to show love to our neighbor. We pray, lead us to share with them the Good News that You gave up Your glory and power in order to sacrifice Your life for us. Thank You for this amazing gift. Amen.

Introduction

Read aloud the opening sentence. Then provide participants an opportunity to discuss the questions that follow. If your class is large, you may want to assign participants to small groups so that all people have an opportunity to share.

1. Answers will vary. Often when someone has done something cruel to someone else and something bad happens to the cruel person, the victim will say, "The tables are turned."

2. We were doomed to eternal death. Jesus' death on the cross won for us eternal life. By God's grace through faith in Jesus we receive the blessings of forgiveness of sins and eternal life.

Read aloud the closing paragraph of this section.

Study

Read aloud or invite volunteers to read aloud portions of Matthew 26:57–66 and the commentary.

Discussing the Text

1. Answers will vary. Probably John would have felt discouraged throughout the night. Perhaps he would have been most hopeful after the hearing before Annas and the first hearing before Pilate. Certainly John would have experienced his greatest despair after Pilate passed the sentence of death.

2. Note the limited number of Sanhedrin members present, the illegal time of trial, the false witnesses, and so forth. Caiaphas was willing to do whatever he could to attain a conviction. God allowed this to happen so His Son could sacrifice His life for us.

3. The purposes of the hearing before Caiaphas were (1) to ease the consciences of as many spiritual leaders as possible and (2) to find charges that would carry the death sentence in the Roman court.

4. Jesus' response, "Yes, it is as you say," is an emphatic statement pointing out that Caiaphas has known all along that Jesus is the Christ, the Son of God. Jesus' response causes Caiaphas to pronounce the verdict, "He has spoken blasphemy!"

5. Caiaphas' verdict was blasphemy, for which the punishment was death.

6. Jesus was taken to Pilate because under Roman law only a Roman official could execute a person.

Apply

Read aloud or invite a volunteer to read aloud the opening two paragraphs. Then discuss the questions that follow.

1. We may stand from a distance, shaking our heads in disgust at the words and actions of Annas, Caiaphas, Pilate, and Herod. But we must realize that Jesus willingly endured humiliation and ultimately suffered and died for only one reason—our sin. It was our sin that brought Jesus to earth. It was our sin that caused Jesus to endure the humiliation of a human court. It was our sin for which Jesus willingly went to the cross to die.

2. When Jesus stood before the judge in our place, He willingly accepted every charge against us. He accepted and endured the death penalty that we deserve because of our sin. We receive the blessings of forgiveness of sins and eternal life through His passive obedience.

3. We can come before God knowing that He accepted Jesus' sacrifice for our sin. We can confidently approach God in worship and prayer. We look forward to the eternal life Jesus won for us that we will experience with God in heaven.

4. We have comfort and hope because we are assured through faith that by Jesus' death we have received the gift of eternal life.

5. Each of these passages reveals how the tables were turned; Jesus suffered what we deserve so that we may receive eternal life.

6. Answers will vary. Obviously, God wants us to know the way to salvation!

Catechism Connection

1. The witnesses gave false testimony about Jesus.

2. Jonathan spoke well of David, and Saul relented on his command to kill David.

3. Love for others—love motivated by God's love for us—leads us to want to speak well of them.

Send

Urge participants to complete one or more of the "Family Connection" activities and one or more of the suggested "For Personal Reflection" activities prior to the next time the class meets. Then close with prayer

For Next Week

Urge participants to read Matthew 28:1–10; John 20:1–18; Acts 10:34–43; and Colossians 3:1–4 in preparation for the next session.

Session 4

Jesus Rises from the Dead

(Matthew 28:1–10; John 20:1–18; Acts 10:34–43;
Colossians 3:1–4)

Gather

Theme: Do Not Be Afraid!

Key Point and Objectives

Invite volunteers to read aloud the key point and each of the objectives.

Opening

Sing or speak together the first two stanzas of "I Know That My Redeemer Lives." Then lead the group in prayer: Thank You, dear Jesus, for rescuing us from eternal damnation through Your death on the cross and for assuring us of victory over death through Your resurrection. Send Your Spirit, we pray, to keep us in the faith so that we can look forward to eternal life with You in heaven. In Your name we pray. Amen.

Introduction

Discuss the questions included in this section. If your class is large, you may wish to assign participants to small groups so that all people have a chance to share.

1. Answers will vary.

2. Answers will vary. People will try to ignore death by referring to death as "passing away" or to the dead person as having "left us." People will try to reverse the process of aging—therefore removing the ultimate result of aging (death) by using cosmetics to cover up wrinkles and undergoing surgical procedures to cosmetically improve body parts. People will often avoid others who have recently experienced the loss of a loved one.

3. We as Christians are assured through faith that we will live forever with Jesus in heaven. We have nothing to fear, for we know that physical death is simply an entry into eternal life.

Read aloud the closing paragraph.

Study

Read aloud or skim Matthew 28:1–10; John 20:1–18; Acts 10:34–43; Colossians 3:1–4 and the commentary. If time is short, you may want to divide the class into small groups and assign each group one of the Bible references. Then provide each group an opportunity to summarize for the entire class what is taught in each of the portions of Scripture.

Discussing the Text

1. *Matthew's account*: Jesus had been laid in the tomb of Joseph of Arimathea; the guards kept watch over the sealed tomb where Jesus' dead body had been laid; at His resurrection the soul of Jesus was reunited with His body; at sunset, women prepared spices to perfume Jesus' decaying body; an angel descended and an earthquake rolled away the stone in front of the tomb; the women approaching the tomb were met by an angel outside the tomb; the angel assured the women that (1) Jesus is risen, (2) Jesus' resurrection is according to His word, (3) because Jesus is risen, there is no reason to be afraid, and (4) the witnesses of Christ's resurrection have something important to share.

John's account: It was still dark when the women set out for the tomb; Mary Magdalene, seeing the stone rolled away, turned and ran back to tell Peter and John; the disciples hurried to the tomb and found the grave cloth neatly folded (obviously, not the work of grave robbers); Scripture has presented sufficient proof that all that happened was as promised; Mary did not tremble with fear at the appearance of the angels; Jesus spoke to Mary; Jesus instructed Mary to go and tell; John's account records few of the angels' words.

2. By Hebrew counting, Sunday morning was the third day. Since the Jewish people counted days beginning with the current one, Friday had been day one. From sundown Friday until sunset Saturday (the Sabbath) Christ's body remained lifeless (day two).

Since the Jews considered evening to be the beginning of a new day, when the sun set on Saturday was the beginning of day three.

3. The angels' message in Matthew and the events in the account included in John's gospel emphasize (1) Jesus is risen, (2) Jesus' resurrection is according to His word, (3) because Jesus is risen there is no reason to be afraid, and (4) the witnesses of Christ's resurrection have something important to share.

4. God directs us to respond to Good News with the message, "Go and tell"; let people know about the salvation Jesus has earned for them!

5. After telling the people that Jesus died and rose again, Peter proclaimed that everyone who believes in Him receives forgiveness of sins through His name.

Apply

Read aloud or invite volunteers to read aloud this section. Then discuss the questions that follow.

1. Jesus' resurrection proved that His work of redemption was complete. The resurrection provides proof that God accepted the sacrifice of Jesus for the sins of all people.

2. Jesus' resurrection proved that (1) Jesus is the Son of God, (2) everything Jesus said was true, (3) God the Father has accepted Christ's death as a sufficient sacrifice for the sins of the world, and (4) we will rise someday, too. Participants might simply share their own faith, pray with the people, pray for the people, share verses and thoughts from Scripture, and the like.

3. Answers will vary. Invite volunteers to share what Jesus' resurrection means to them.

4. Answers will vary.

Catechism Connection

1. Paul reveals that believers died (verse 3a), have been raised (1a), and have taken off their old selves (9b).

2. Paul directs believers to set their minds on things above (verse 2) and to put to death practices that belong to their earthly nature (verses 5 and 8).

3. Answers will vary. Paul calls on believers to become in daily practice what we are through God's grace in Christ.

Send

Urge participants to complete one or more of the suggested "Family Connection" activities and one or more of the suggested "For Personal Reflection" activities prior to the next time the class meets. Then close with prayer.

For Next Week

Urge participants to read John 20:19–31; Acts 2:14–41; 4:1–31; and 1 Peter 1:3–9 in preparation for the next session.

Session 5

We Know That Jesus Rose from the Dead

(John 20:19–31; Acts 2:14–41; 4:1–31; 1 Peter 1:3–9)

— Gather —

Theme: Peace

Key Point and Objectives

Invite different volunteers to read aloud the key point and each of the objectives.

Opening

Speak together the words of the hymn "Christ Is Arisen." Then lead the group in prayer (adapted from *The Lutheran Hymnal*): Grant, we beseech You, Almighty God, that we who have celebrated the solemnities of the Lord's resurrection may, by the help of Your grace, bring forth fruits thereof in our life and conversation; through the same Jesus Christ, Your Son, our Lord. Amen.

Introduction

Discuss the questions included in this section. If your class is large, you may want to assign participants to small groups so that all individuals have a chance to share.

1. Answers will vary. If possible, write participants' responses on newsprint or an overhead transparency so you can underline and circle them together as a class as suggested in questions 2 and 3.

2. Peace as the world would explain it would be the absence of fear, war, troubles, and hardships.

3. Peace as God can provide it is the peace that comes from knowing that through faith in Jesus we have received the gift of forgiveness of sins and eternal life.

4. Answers will vary. The world's view of peace focuses on physical life. God's view of peace focuses on our spiritual life, through the gift of eternal life.

Read aloud the closing paragraph of this section.

Study

Read aloud or skim John 20:19–31; Acts 2:14–41; 4:1–31; 1 Peter 1:3–9; and the commentary.

Discussing the Text

1. For anyone to benefit from Jesus' resurrection it had to be known, believed, and proclaimed. Jesus' resurrection provided proof that the sacrificial death of Jesus on the cross was a sufficient payment for the sins of the world.

2. Whether uneasy about our personal safety or about our eternal welfare, the Gospel brings peace—*shalom:* the condition of total well-being that we enjoy when we are in a whole relationship with God.

3. The mission of the apostles is to forgive sins. Forgiveness of sins is the essence of the Christian message—for Jesus won forgiveness of sins through His death on the cross.

4. The biblical accounts of the resurrection have a solid historical foundation. More eyewitnesses of this event have recorded their personal testimonies than have recorded any other historical event. Paul records that most of the more than 500 witnesses of the resurrected Lord were still alive when he wrote 1 Corinthians. Jesus' enemies provide evidence of His resurrection. Some writers of the second century continued to report that Jesus' disciples had stolen the body. This verifies that the grave was indeed empty.

5. Christ's disciples were transformed from cowering deserters to fearless preachers of the faith. This is proof of the resurrection. Since many of the apostles and other followers of Jesus were persecuted and put to death for their convictions, we must assume that they were certain of the resurrection.

Apply

Read aloud or invite volunteers to read aloud the opening paragraphs in this section. Then discuss the questions that follow.

1. Answers will vary. We no longer need to fear death for we will share in the victory Jesus won for us over death. We will live forever with God in heaven. Christ's death and resurrection form the basis of faith.

2. The apostolic progression is passed down from generation to generation as pastors are ordained into the holy ministry. The Christian church continues to do that which Jesus commissioned it to do—to forgive sins. When we hear forgiveness proclaimed and announced during worship, we can be certain that Jesus Himself speaks.

3. Jesus was patient with Thomas. He is patient with doubters today. All of us will at times doubt our faith. As Jesus dealt gently with Peter, so He deals patiently with us today.

4. Jesus' appearance on Easter gives some hints as to the nature of our bodies in the resurrection from the dead. In heaven we will still be ourselves—fully human, real and physical, with the same bodies we now have, but glorified.

5. As we demonstrate our faith even as we face trials and tribulations, we have the opportunity to "give the reason for the hope that [we] have" (1 Peter 3:15).

6. Following this account, John places everything in perspective: Believing that the crucified and risen Savior is the Christ, the Son of God, is **THE** one means by which we are saved.

Catechism Connection

1. Answers will vary. Faith in Christ leads to a changed life.

2. When God saved us, He expected a changed life to follow—a life empowered by His saving actions for us.

3. As we received faith in Christ, our old self was "crucified with Him." In its place God gave us a new nature that desires to serve Him.

Send

Urge participants to complete one or more of the suggested "Family Connection" activities and one or more of the suggested "For Personal Reflection" activities prior to the next time the class meets. Then close with prayer.

For Next Week

Urge participants to read Luke 24:13–35 in preparation for the next session.

Session 6

Jesus Appears to Two Disciples

(Luke 24:13–35)

Gather

Theme: An Eyewitness

Key Point and Objectives

Invite volunteers to read aloud the key point and each of the objectives.

Opening

Read the printed portions of Luther's explanations of the Lord's Supper responsively. Then lead the group in prayer: Dear Savior, as You opened the eyes of two disciples through the breaking of bread, so use this Sacrament to strengthen our faith. Finally, bring us to live with You forever in our eternal home. We pray in Your name. Amen.

Introduction

Discuss the questions in this section. If your class is large, you may want to assign participants to small groups so that each individual has an opportunity to share.

1. Answers will vary. An eyewitness account adds credibility to an event's occurrence. It makes the event come alive for those with whom the eyewitness shares the event.

2. Eyewitness accounts of the resurrection emphasize the truth of the event. The eyewitness accounts of the resurrection add credibility to its truth.

3. God reveals to us the truth of the resurrection in Scripture. God's Word provides a reliable and truthful account of the events preceding, including, and following the resurrection.

Read aloud or invite a volunteer to read aloud the closing paragraph of this section.

Study

Read aloud Luke 24:13–35 and the commentary.

Discussing the Text

1. Jesus emphasized to the disciples on the road to Emmaus that the written Word of God provided all they needed to know about the person and work of Jesus. Jesus teaches that His disciples can discover all they need to know in God's Word in order to believe.

2. The disciples would need to understand how Jesus fulfilled the Old Testament prophecies. Imagine the "Bible studies" Cleopas and his traveling companion must have led during the days that followed!

3. The disciples should have expected the events that had occurred during the last few days, for Jesus had revealed to His disciples that He would die for the sins of all people. Rather than being a setback, the events of the last few days had actually fulfilled God's plan.

4. The breaking of the bread reminded the disciples of the Lord's Supper, in which Jesus would continue to be physically present with His church.

5. The disciples had seen, had heard, and had eaten with the risen Jesus. Jesus revealed the truth concerning the resurrection through Scripture. This was important for Jesus to do so that the disciples and we would know that we can rely on Scripture as God's truth.

6. The disciples were excited and eager to share Good News. Imagine how such excitement and eagerness would affect the way we share the Gospel today!

Apply

Read aloud the opening paragraphs of this section. Then discuss the questions that follow.

1. While we are not technically eyewitnesses of the resurrection, Scripture reveals all that we need to know about the person and work of Jesus. Jesus reveals to us His purpose and His work on our behalf as He did with the disciples on the road to Emmaus—by sharing His Word.

2. The purpose of all Scripture is to reveal God's plan of salvation fulfilled in the person and work of Jesus on our behalf.

3. Answers will vary. Looking for Christ on every page of Scripture would enable us to (1) tap into the faith-strengthening power of the Holy Spirit working through God's Word, (2) interpret God's Word with wisdom, and (3) share God's Word more effectively with others.

Catechism Connection

1. Christ's words are a testament that must be taken at face value. The bread and wine in the Sacrament are a communion or participation in the body and blood of Christ.

2. Christ made one sacrifice for sin, not many sacrifices.

3. The Sacrament assures us that, dead to sin, we may live for righteousness. Thus, we receive strength for our Christian life.

Send

Urge participants to complete one or more of the "Family Connection" activities and one or more of the suggested "For Personal Reflection" activities prior to the next time the class meets. Then close with prayer.

For Next Week

Urge participants to read Acts 6:1–8:1 in preparation for the next session.

Session 7

Stephen Tells about Jesus

(Acts 6:1–8:1)

Gather

Theme: A Martyr!

Key Point and Objectives

Invite different volunteers to read aloud the key point and each of the objectives.

Opening

Read the Fifth Petition and Luther's explanation responsively. Then lead the group in prayer: Father, we confess that at times we fail to proclaim Your love during times of persecution, rejection, or disapproval because of our Christian faith. Forgive us, we pray, and work through such experiences to strengthen our faith. We pray in Jesus' name. Amen.

Introduction

Discuss the questions included in this section. If your class is large, you may want to assign participants to small groups so that all have an opportunity to share.

1. Answers will vary. Remind participants that persecution often takes a more subtle form than fearing for your life and fearing for your safety.

2. Answers will vary.

Read aloud the closing paragraph of this section.

Study

Invite volunteers to read aloud portions of Acts 6:1–8:1 and the commentary.

Discussing the Text

1. The Hellenist Jews complained against the Hebrew Jews because the widows of the Hellenist Jews were being overlooked in the daily distribution of food. The 12 apostles gathered to come up with a solution. They decided to appoint seven men who would be responsible for the distribution of food. The seven were to administer the temporal matters of the church.

2. Stephen was very effective in his witnessing. The religious leaders from the synagogue became jealous of his effectiveness and created charges to bring him before the Sanhedrin.

3. Like Jesus' trial, Stephen's trial was before the Sanhedrin. False witnesses were called, and similar charges were brought against Stephen as had been brought against Jesus. Unlike Jesus, Stephen provided a lengthy defense for himself.

4. Stephen recounts the long history of Israel beginning with Abraham and how the Israelites had rejected God and His Word throughout history. Stephen points out that just as Israel had constantly rejected God's spokesmen, this generation has betrayed and killed "the Righteous One," the Messiah.

5. The Jewish people considered Abraham as their father. God promised blessings through Abraham's seed—through Jesus—but Stephen's accusers still thought that promise would be fulfilled through an earthly kingdom.

6. Answers will vary. In Stephen's answer we find a summary of key Old Testament events, and we see how God was at work to save the world through Christ.

7. The Sanhedrin reacted violently to Stephen's accusation that they had murdered Jesus. The Sanhedrin accused Stephen of blasphemy, the same charge brought against Jesus.

8. Stephen says, "Lord Jesus, receive my spirit" and "Lord, do not hold this sin against them." These words are similar to Jesus' words spoken from the cross.

Apply

Read aloud or invite a volunteer to read aloud the opening paragraphs of this section. Then discuss the questions that follow.

1. Answers will vary. Pressure, ridicule, and abandonment are more subtle forms of persecution that people may be subjected to today.

2. Jesus suffered on our behalf on the cross. We sometimes endure persecution because of our relationship with Him. Therefore, we share in His suffering.

3. With persecution comes the promise of Christ's presence to deliver us. When facing persecution, Christians often cling more heartily to the Word of God through which the Holy Spirit works to strengthen faith. This in turn causes Christians to proclaim more boldly God's love for them revealed in the person and work of Jesus.

4. Answers will vary. Throughout history after the death of a martyr, the Christian church is strengthened and often witnesses for Jesus Christ crucified with greater zeal.

5. Answers will vary.

6. Answers will vary.

Catechism Connection

1. Peter said that God exalted Jesus "to His own right hand as Prince and Savior that He might give repentance and forgiveness of sins to Israel" (Acts 5:31).

2. We can forgive others because through Christ God has forgiven us. Raised with Christ, we are able to set our minds on things above.

3. Answers will vary.

Send

Urge participants to complete one or more of the "Family Connection" activities and one or more of the "For Personal Reflection" activities prior to the next time the class meets. Then close with prayer.

For Next Week

Urge participants to read Acts 17:1–34 and 23:12–35 in preparation for the next session.

Session 8

Paul Proclaims the Gospel

(Acts 17:1–34; 23:12–35)

Gather

Theme: Empty

Key Point and Objectives

Invite different volunteers to read aloud the key point and each of the objectives.

Opening

Read the First Commandment and Luther's explanation responsively. Then lead the group in prayer: Dear Jesus, even though You deserved all the privileges of being true God, You humbled Yourself, took the form of a servant, and suffered the punishment we deserve because of our sins. Strengthen us, we pray, so that we will always humble ourselves and give You first place in our lives. In Your name we pray. Amen.

Introduction

Read aloud with feeling the statement "I feel empty inside." Then discuss the questions that follow. If your class is large, you may want to assign participants to small groups so that all have an opportunity to share.

1. Answers will vary. We may speak these words after a long day, after facing a trying ordeal, or after ministering to the needs of a loved one.

2. Answers will vary. People attempt to fill their emptiness with drugs, alcohol, sex, the acquisition of things, their job, and so forth.

Read aloud the closing paragraph of this section.

Study

Read aloud or invite volunteers to read aloud portions of Acts 17:1–34; 23:12–35; and the commentary.

Discussing the Text

1. Paul encountered the Athenians in the marketplace, called the agora. Paul typically began his ministry in a synagogue in a town or city. But he recognized that in Athens the marketplace was the center of philosophic and religious discussion. The Athenians were not impressed with Paul, but they were intrigued enough to invite him to address the Areopagus.

2. Paul abandons his typical methods so that he can appeal to the Athenians. Although his message to the Athenians focuses on Jesus Christ, his method of sharing the message is different than the typical method he uses. Paul employs the style of argumentation familiar to the Athenians, beginning with an illustration that the Athenians could relate to.

3. The discussion ends abruptly. The resurrection is absurd to the Athenians. Most sneer at Paul's message. Others remain interested in what Paul had to say, but unmoved. A few do come to faith.

4. In 1 Corinthians 1 Paul does not appeal to human wisdom. Rather, he simply preaches "Christ crucified" (1:23).

5. Angry Jews accused Paul of desecrating the temple by bringing Gentiles into it, an offense for which the Romans would permit the Jews to execute a man. Paul was taken into protective custody by the Roman commander.

6. Paul's nephew hears of the plot to murder Paul. His nephew tells the Roman commander. The commander sends Paul to the Roman governor, Felix, in Caesarea. An entourage of soldiers escorts Paul out of Jerusalem.

7. Answers will vary. It is evident that God uses hardships, threats, and persecution to further His kingdom through the work of Paul.

Apply

Read aloud or invite volunteers to read aloud the opening paragraphs of this section. Then discuss the questions that follow.

1. "Know your audience." This is not simply a cliché. Instead, it is important that we know our audience so that the message we wish to share has the greatest impact. We need to relate to our audiences' experiences so that our hearers will better understand our message. This is important for us as individuals who desire that our witness of faith has an impact on others' lives. This is also important for Christian congregations that wish to effectively reach out to their communities. We are reminded of Paul's words to the Christian congregation in Corinth: "I have become all things to all men so that by all possible means I might save some. I do all this for the sake of the gospel, that I may share in its blessings" (1 Corinthians 9:22–23).

2. We do not convert unbelievers, nor does God call upon us to convert unbelievers. Instead, God calls us to share the Gospel through which the Holy Spirit works to create and to strengthen saving faith in Jesus. The Athenians' response to Paul's message may be the response we initially receive from unbelievers. But remember, the Holy Spirit will continue to work on the hearts of those who hear the message of God's love through Jesus Christ.

3. Answers will vary. Without Jesus, people live without the hope of eternal life that only Jesus can assure. This leads to a search to fill the emptiness caused by unanswered questions, primarily the one the rich young man asked Jesus: "Teacher, what good thing must I do to get eternal life?" (Matthew 19:16).

4. Answers will vary.

Catechism Connection

1. We bow our knee at the name of Jesus and confess Jesus Christ as Lord.

2. We consider others better than ourselves, looking for ways to help them.

3. We have the love of Christ and fellowship with the Spirit.

Send

Urge participants to complete one or more of the "Family Connection" activities and one or more of the suggested "For Personal Reflection" activities during the next week. Then close with prayer.

For Next Week

Urge participants to read Acts 27:1–28:31 in preparation for the next session.

Session 9

God Preserves Paul from a Shipwreck

(Acts 27:1–28:31)

Gather

Theme: Who's in Control?

Key Point and Objectives

Invite different volunteers to read aloud the key point and each of the objectives.

Opening

Read Luther's explanation of the benefits of Baptism responsively. Then lead the group in prayer: Heavenly Father, when problems of life threaten to overwhelm us, remind us that You saved us by the waters of Holy Baptism. May we always trust Your care and protection. Hear us for Jesus' sake. Amen.

Introduction

Read aloud the quote from the popular bumper sticker. Then have participants discuss the questions that follow. If your class is large, you may want to assign participants to small groups to discuss the questions so that all participants have a chance to share.

1. Answers will vary. The truth is God doesn't move. We do! If we sense God is distant, we can always turn to His Word—it remains unchanging and unmoving. Through God's Word, the Holy Spirit works to strengthen our faith in Jesus, thereby strengthening our relationship with God.

2. Answers will vary. Invite participants to share.

Read aloud the closing paragraph of this section.

Study

Invite volunteers to read aloud portions of Acts 27:1–28:31 and the commentary.

Discussing the Text

1. After two years in detention under Felix, the new governor Festus wanted Paul to return to Jerusalem to stand trial before the Jews. Knowing the danger that faced him in Jerusalem, Paul exercised his right as a Roman citizen and appealed to Caesar. The governor was obligated to honor Paul's request. The government would finance Paul's journey to Rome.

2. A sudden wind of hurricane force swept down the mountains and into the sea. After two weeks out of control, the crew sensed it was near land. The ship ran aground and was quickly smashed by the waves. The prisoners and crew swam to shore; all 276 people made it to safety.

3. Miraculously, no one was harmed during the storm or in the swim to land. God's hand was evident throughout the experience.

4. The miraculous survival of those on the ship provided open ears for Paul's preaching of Christ. Every time the crew landed at another port, Paul would preach Jesus Christ crucified and risen.

5. God gave peace to Paul and led him to eat and to thank God for the food. Paul's words and example encouraged the others.

6. Some responded to the Gospel by turning to faith, but others resisted.

7. The book of Acts closes with the same great optimism with which it began. The Gospel will continue to go out to all nations, just as Jesus Himself had promised. The book of Acts really has no ending. Instead, the history of the Christian church is a story that has continued for centuries and will continue for centuries to come.

Apply

Invite volunteers to read aloud the two paragraphs in this section. Then discuss the questions that follow.

1. God's action in saving those on the ship provides a vivid illustration of God's constant protection. God always guards His people

from physical danger. More important, God constantly guards His people from spiritual threats from the devil.

2. God's Word will go out with its saving message and power wherever and whenever He intends. God was able to use the frightening experience of the shipwreck as an opportunity for Paul to share the Good News of Jesus Christ with people who might not have heard it otherwise.

3. Answers will vary. Be sensitive to the fact that often when God opens a door, we may close it because of sin and fear. Share the Good News that Jesus went to the cross to forgive us from all sins, including the times when we fail to share His love and forgiveness with others.

4. Answers will vary. We will recognize that any event, situation, or person we encounter may be God providing us a new opportunity to share our faith.

5. God's Word is powerful. We can be confident that God is working through His Word, even though we may not see the results.

Catechism Connection

1. The shipwreck provided opportunities for Paul to share the Gospel. As a result, many were saved from eternal damnation.

2. God's kindness (in this case, the salvation He works through Baptism) leads to repentance.

3. For adults, both repentance and Baptism are gifts we receive through the Gospel, which Peter proclaimed in the preceding verses.

Send

Urge participants to complete one or more of the "Family Connection" activities and one or more of the "For Personal Reflection" activities prior to the next time the class meets. Then close with prayer.

For Next Week

Urge participants to read Acts 1:1–14 in preparation for the next session.

Session 10

Jesus Ascends into Heaven

(Acts 1:1–14)

Gather

Theme: God's Itinerary

Key Point and Objectives

Invite different volunteers to read aloud the key point and each of the objectives.

Opening

Pray together the Collect for the Ascension of Our Lord.

Introduction

Read aloud the opening paragraph. Then discuss the questions that follow. If your class is large, you may want to assign participants to small groups so that all people have the opportunity to share their responses.

1. Answers will vary.

2. Answers will vary. Sometimes as we follow our itinerary rather than God's, we face hardships and troubles as consequences. Sometimes, though, even as we follow God's itinerary, we will face troubles and hardships. This simply is a result of sin in this world. When our itinerary leads us away from God, we may face the consequence of feeling distant from God, alone, or helpless. At these times God calls us through the Gospel to turn away from our sin to Him so that we might receive the forgiveness Jesus won for us on the cross.

3. Answers will vary.

Study

Read aloud Acts 1:1–14. Then invite volunteers to read aloud portions of the commentary.

Discussing the Text

1. Jesus commands His followers not to leave Jerusalem, for in Jerusalem on the day of Pentecost they will receive the Holy Spirit.

2. Answers will vary. Still somewhat unclear about their mission, perhaps many would have returned to their own homes.

3. The disciples ask, "Lord, are You at this time going to restore the kingdom to Israel?" The disciples still wonder if Jesus' purpose was to come to earth to restore the nation of Israel.

4. Jesus gently corrects His disciples by pointing to a higher goal—taking the salvation He won to the world.

5. Jesus maps out the itinerary for the entire book of Acts. They will begin by sharing His message of forgiveness close to home (Jerusalem), then in the surrounding regions (Judea and Samaria), and finally to the ends of the earth.

6. The two "men" in white reminded the disciples that Jesus would return physically and visibly.

7. Answers will vary. Jesus reassured the disciples by promising the Holy Spirit and by sending two angels to speak with them. His physical ascent into heaven assured them that He really is God, ruling and blessing His church.

8. The ascended Jesus is crowned with glory and honor. The angels are His ministering servants.

Apply

Read aloud the opening paragraphs of this section. Then discuss the questions that follow.

1. Jesus enters heaven as our forerunner. We are assured that just as Jesus was received into the glory of heaven, we, too, will ascend into heaven one day.

2. Jesus is with us everywhere, at every moment. He is always present—both in His divinity and in His humanity. Jesus is no longer bound by time and space. He is truly with us always.

3. In the Lord's Supper, Jesus' body and blood are really present in, with, and under the bread and the wine. The Lord's Supper assures us of Jesus' presence with us.

4. Jesus constantly intercedes for us and all believers. Also, the ascended Christ rules over all things on earth, including our lives, for the good of His church.

5. Answers will vary.

Catechism Connection

1. Jesus has complete authority; He is the head of His church.

2. He works through people whom He has appointed to carry out His work—evangelists, pastors, teachers, and so forth.

3. Jesus has sent the Counselor—the Holy Spirit, whom He had promised—to give us the strength to carry out His work.

Send

Urge participants to complete one or more of the "Family Connection" activities and one or more of the "For Personal Reflection" activities prior to the next time the class meets. Then close with prayer.

For Next Week

Urge participants to read Acts 2:1–41; Joel 2:28–29; and John 16:5–11 in preparation for the next session.

Session 11

The Holy Spirit Comes

(Acts 2:1–41; Joel 2:28–29; John 16:5–11)

Gather

Theme: Transformation

Key Point and Objectives

Invite different volunteers to read aloud the key point and each of the objectives.

Opening

Read the Third Article and Luther's explanation responsively. Then lead the group in prayer: Thank You, dear Father, for rescuing us from sin through Your Son, Jesus, and for bringing us to faith in Him by the power of the Holy Spirit. We pray, continue to pour out Your Spirit upon us, empowering us to share our faith with people lost in sin. Hear us for Jesus' sake. Amen.

Introduction

Ask participants to reflect upon the transforming work of the Holy Spirit. Remind participants that the Holy Spirit continues to work mightily today through Word and Sacrament to create and to strengthen saving faith.

Read aloud this section. Invite participants to respond to ideas presented in this section.

Study

Read aloud or invite volunteers to read aloud portions of Acts 2:1–41; John 15:5–11; and the commentary.

Discussing the Text

1. Following God's command, the Jewish people gathered at the Feast of Weeks, or the Feast of Harvest. Pentecost was a kind of firstfruits thanksgiving at the time of the early wheat harvest, 50 days after Passover. The word *pentecost* comes from the Greek and means "fiftieth." The celebration attracted to Jerusalem thousands of Jewish visitors "from every nation under heaven" (Acts 2:5).

2. The Hebrew word for *wind* or *breath* is the same word as *spirit*, and fire was associated with the Holy Spirit.

3. The gift of the believers to speak in foreign languages they had never learned was the most apparent gift received on the day of Pentecost. The gift of "speaking in tongues," however, involves speaking in unrecognizable languages. The audience on the day of Pentecost clearly recognized and understood the languages being spoken.

4. This was not a haphazard event. Peter was pointing out how God was fulfilling the prophecy He gave through Joel.

5. Peter's sermon develops around the following four assertions: (1) by many miracles God testified to Jesus of Nazareth (2:22); (2) Jesus' suffering was according to God's plan (2:23a); (3) "you" crucified Him (2:23b); and (4) God raised Jesus from the dead and exalted Him to His throne of grace in heaven (2:24–36).

6. Peter's message of Law and Gospel had its desired effect. The people were ready to respond to God's grace.

7. The preaching of the Word, empowered by the Holy Spirit, was powerful—3,000 people received the gift of saving faith in Christ Jesus.

Apply

Read aloud or invite volunteers to read aloud the opening paragraphs of this section. Then discuss the questions that follow.

1. By the power of the Holy Spirit, cowering disciples were transformed into fearless and bold witnesses of the Gospel. The Holy Spirit working through God's Word on the day of Pentecost caused 3,000 people to become believers. On our Baptism, the Holy Spirit transformed us from God's enemies to heirs of heaven. Through Holy Baptism God claimed you as His own.

2. The Holy Spirit enables and empowers us to confess our faith to all people. The Holy Spirit works through our sharing of the Gospel to melt the resistance of those to whom we speak.

3. As we repent, Jesus forgives even our worst sins. If God forgave people for murdering Jesus, He will also forgive our sins for Jesus' sake.

4. The Christian church was born by the Holy Spirit. As God's children claimed by the power of the Holy Spirit in Holy Baptism, we are members of His church—both the church present now on earth and those who rest with Jesus in heaven.

5. Answers will vary.

Catechism Connection

1. The Holy Spirit brings us into the church, which becomes our teacher—which leads us to Christ.

2. The Holy Spirit leads us to live a God-pleasing life.

3. Even when we fail to pray, the Holy Spirit intercedes for us.

Send

Urge participants to complete one or more of the "Family Connection" activities and one or more of the "For Personal Reflection" activities prior to the next time the class meets. Then close with prayer.

For Next Week

Urge participants to read Matthew 25:31–46 and Matthew 28:16–20 in preparation for the next session.

Session 12

Jesus Will Take Us to Heaven

(Matthew 25:31–46; 28:16–20)

Gather

Theme: Celebrate!

Key Point and Objectives

Invite different volunteers to read aloud the key point and each of the objectives.

Opening

Read the Apostles' Creed together. Then lead the group in the prayer: Almighty and everlasting God, by Your grace we acknowledge the glory of the eternal Trinity and we worship the true Unity in the power of Your divine majesty. We pray, keep us steadfast in this true faith and worship, and defend us ever from all our adversaries; for You, O Father, Son, and Holy Spirit, live and reign, one God, now and forever. Amen.

Introduction

Discuss the questions included in this section. If the class is large, you may want to assign participants to small groups so that all get a chance to share.

1. Answers will vary. Possible responses might include birthdays, anniversaries, retirements, and so forth.

2. Again, answers will vary.

3. Answers will vary. Some might be very surprised with a celebration for the coming of Judgment Day. Many people fear Judgment Day and therefore would never think of celebrating it.

Read aloud the closing paragraph of this section.

Study

Invite volunteers to read aloud Matthew 25:31–46; 28:16–20; and the commentary.

Discussing the Text

1. Jesus will return when He is least expected. We must be ready at all times.

2. At the moment when He is least expected, Jesus will physically and visibly descend from the clouds of heaven and take His seat on the throne of judgment. Angels will trumpet His return to earth. All people, both the living and the dead, will be gathered before Him. Jesus will separate all the people into two groups—those who possess saving faith and those who do not.

3. The metaphor of sheep and goats recalls Jesus' role as the Good Shepherd who died to save the sheep. Sheep possess saving faith. Goats are unbelievers.

4. Good works are evidence of faith. Faith in Jesus motivates believers to do good works. Lack of faith makes it impossible for a person to do anything truly good. Good works by an unbeliever are worthless before God because they come from sinful, corrupt hearts. Everything unbelievers do is sin.

5. People receive an inheritance based upon who they are, not on what they do. The good works are fruits of faith.

6. The Great Commission is fulfilled by Christ. Through Baptism, Jesus brings new souls into the family of God, giving them His name—Christian. Remember, Jesus is God's Word become flesh. As we teach God's Word, the Holy Spirit works to strengthen our faith in Jesus. When Christ's Word is taught, Christ Himself is speaking.

7. Jesus remains with His church today through the means of grace—the Word and the Sacraments.

Apply

Read aloud or invite a volunteer to read aloud the opening paragraphs of this section. Then discuss the questions that follow.

1. We desire that all people experience the joy we will experience with Jesus in eternity. Since no one knows the time when Jesus will

return, there is an urgency to share the Gospel with friends and loved ones. We desire that they be with us someday in heaven.

2. For believers, Judgment Day will be a glorious experience. We will rise to live with Jesus forever in heaven.

3. We respond to Jesus' love for us by doing good works for others. When we serve others in faith, we serve Jesus.

4. Jesus' presence with us becomes tangible in the means of grace—Word and Sacraments. He is not "with you always" in some vague sense. Instead, He is speaking when the pastor speaks, touching us with water in Baptism, and giving us His body and blood in bread and wine to eat and to drink. Jesus provides forgiveness, guidance, and eternal life to us through these means.

5. Paul begins and ends this section with references to the return of Christ, where believers will receive their promised inheritance. In the intervening verses he emphasizes sharing the Gospel and remaining faithful to it—the task God gives us today.

Catechism Connection

1. God the Father, Jesus Christ, and the Holy Spirit form the Trinity—three distinct persons in one divine being.

2. God the Father is our Creator, Jesus is our Redeemer, and the Holy Spirit is our Sanctifier.

3. The Creed must be faithful to Scripture so that it, too, will reveal the way to salvation.

Send

Urge participants to complete one or more of the "Family Connection" activities and one or more of the "For Personal Reflection" activities prior to the next time the class meets. Then close with prayer.

For Next Week

Urge participants to read Luke 10:1–24 and Matthew 5:13–20 in preparation for the next session.

Session 13

Jesus Sends Workers into His Harvest Field

(Luke 10:1–24; Matthew 5:13–20)

Gather

Theme: Equipped

Read aloud the theme. Then ask, "For what are you equipped?" Provide time for volunteers to respond.

Key Point and Objectives

Invite different volunteers to read aloud the key point and each of the objectives.

Opening

Read the Second Petition of the Lord's Prayer and Luther's explanation responsively. Then lead the group in prayer: Almighty God, You have called Your church to witness that in Christ You have reconciled us to Yourself. We pray, grant that by Your Holy Spirit we may proclaim the Good News of Your salvation, that all who hear it may receive the gift of salvation; through Jesus Christ, our Lord. Amen.

Introduction

Read the sentence starter. Then discuss the questions that follow.

1. Answers will vary.

2. Answers will vary.

3. Answers will vary. Don't be surprised if some agree that they are not adequately equipped to share Jesus with others.

Read aloud the closing paragraph of this section.

Study

Read aloud or invite volunteers to read aloud portions of Luke 10:1–24 and Matthew 5:13–20. Then read aloud portions of the commentary. If time is short, you may wish to summarize the important facts included in this commentary.

Discussing the Text

1. Jesus tells us, "Let your light shine before men." Through words and actions we give a witness of His love to us.

2. Jesus selected individuals to serve as workers—to carry His message to others.

3. Seventy was a symbolic number for the whole nation of Israel. Seventy was also the number of elders appointed to assist Moses.

4. The 70 were instructed to go out in the simplest—almost naive—faith, without even basic necessities. They were to trust God fully for all of their needs.

5. The 70 were given the authority to proclaim the same message Jesus and John the Baptist had preached, "The kingdom of God has come near you!" It was a message of both Law and Gospel.

6. Some believed and were saved; others rejected and were damned. The same is true for people today who hear the Word of God.

7. The greatest joy of a disciple is the promise of eternal life with Jesus in heaven. Heaven is the only thing that we can receive that will last into eternity.

Apply

Read aloud or invite volunteers to read aloud the opening paragraphs. Then discuss the questions that follow.

1. Jesus says to all of His disciples, "Let your light shine"; "You will be My witnesses."

2. Answers will vary.

3. Answers will vary. Some will gladly hear the Word of God and receive it. Others will reject the Word. Jesus will continue to equip and empower us for service to Him.

4. Urge participants to write a prayer as directed in the Study Guide.

Catechism Connection

1. Luther says that with the power of the Holy Spirit we believe God's Word and lead godly lives, the same point Jesus makes in Matthew 5:16. God relies on us—by proclaiming the Gospel and by living our lives in ways that bear witness to it—to share the message of salvation with lost souls.

2. God equips us for service through His Word. Through the Word the Holy Spirit reveals the Gospel of salvation and the power for a godly life. God also provides His power through the Sacraments—Baptism and the Lord's Supper.

3. God promises to rescue us and finally to bring us into His heavenly kingdom.

Send

Urge participants to complete one or more of the suggested "Family Connection" activities and one or more of the "For Personal Reflection" activities prior to the next time the class meets. Then close with prayer.